It's another great book from CGP...

GCSE Biology is all about **understanding how science works**.
And not only that — understanding it well enough to be able to **question**
what you hear on TV and read in the papers.

But don't panic. This book includes all the **science facts** you need to learn,
and shows you how they work in the real world. It even includes
a **free** Online Edition you can read on your computer or tablet.

How to get your free Online Edition

Just go to **cgpbooks.co.uk/extras** and enter this code...

2916 5358 8801 9485

By the way, this code only works for one person. If somebody else has used
this book before you, they might have already claimed the Online Edition.

CGP — still the best! ☺

Our sole aim here at CGP is to produce the highest
quality books — carefully written, immaculately presented
and dangerously close to being funny.

Then we work our socks off to get them
out to you — at the cheapest possible prices.

Contents

Published by CGP

From original material by Richard Parsons.

Editors:
Joe Brazier, Emma Elder, Murray Hamilton, Edmund Robinson, Hayley Thompson.

Contributors:
James Foster, Derek Harvey, Adrian Schmit, Sophie Watkins.

ISBN: 978 1 84762 612 7

With thanks to Helen Brace, Charlotte Burrows, Ben Fletcher, Sue Hocking and
Rosie McCurrie for the proofreading.

With thanks to Laura Jakubowski for the copyright research.

Printed by Elanders Ltd, Newcastle upon Tyne.
Clipart from Corel®

The Scientific Process

This section <u>isn't</u> about how to 'do' science — but it does show you the way <u>most scientists</u> work, and how scientists try to find decent <u>explanations</u> for things that happen. It's pretty important stuff.

Scientists Come Up With <u>Hypotheses</u> — <u>Then</u> <u>Test</u> <u>Them</u>

1) Scientists try to <u>explain</u> things. Everything.

2) They start by <u>observing</u> or <u>thinking about</u> something they don't understand — it could be anything, e.g. planets in the sky, a person suffering from an illness, what matter is made of... anything.

3) They then try to come up with a <u>hypothesis</u>:

- A hypothesis <u>isn't</u> just a <u>summary</u> of their observations (e.g. red blood cells are red).

- It's an <u>explanation</u> for it (e.g. red blood cells are red because they contain haemoglobin).

- Observations made by scientists are just that — observations. They <u>don't show</u> what the hypothesis should be. In order to come up with a decent explanation for their observations, scientists need to <u>use their imagination</u>.

- A good hypothesis should account for <u>all</u> of the observations made and any other <u>available data</u> (i.e. what's already been observed). If it doesn't, it's not really a very good explanation.

4) The next step is to <u>test</u> whether the hypothesis might be <u>right or not</u>. This involves making a <u>prediction</u> based on the hypothesis and testing it by <u>gathering evidence</u> (i.e. <u>data</u>) from <u>investigations</u>.

5) If <u>evidence</u> from <u>experiments</u> backs up a prediction, it <u>increases confidence</u> in the <u>hypothesis</u> — in other words, people are more likely to believe that the hypothesis is true. It <u>doesn't prove</u> a hypothesis is <u>correct</u> though — evidence could still be found that <u>disagrees</u> with it.

6) If the experimental evidence <u>doesn't fit</u> with the hypothesis, then either those <u>results</u> or the <u>hypothesis</u> must be <u>wrong</u> — this <u>decreases confidence</u> in the hypothesis.

7) Sometimes a hypothesis will account for all the data and still turn out to be <u>wrong</u> — that's why every hypothesis needs to be <u>tested</u> further (see next page).

Different Scientists <u>Can Come Up With</u> Different Explanations

Observations can pretty much always be explained in <u>more than one way</u>.
Which can make the scientific process a little <u>tricky</u>...

1) Different scientists can make the <u>same observations</u> and come up with <u>different explanations</u> for them — and both these explanations might be perfectly <u>good</u> ones.

2) This is because you need to <u>interpret</u> what you're observing to come up with an explanation, and different people often interpret things in different ways.

3) Sometimes a scientist's <u>personal background</u> will influence the way he or she thinks. For example, a trained geneticist might lean towards a genetic explanation for a particular disease, but someone else might think it's more about the environment.

4) In these situations, it's important to <u>test</u> the explanations as much as possible — to see which one is most likely to be true (or whether it's a combination of both).

Science is a "real-world" subject...

Science isn't just about explaining things that people are curious about. If scientists can explain something that happens in the world, then maybe they can <u>predict</u> what will happen in the future. They might even be able to <u>control future events</u>. This could make life a bit better in some way, either for themselves or for other people.

The Scientific Process

The scientific process can be quite <u>long</u>... which is why there's another page on it.
I bet you just <u>can't wait</u> to see how it ends up. Enjoy.

Several Scientists <u>Will</u> Test a Hypothesis

1) The scientific process depends on '<u>peer review</u>'.
This means that scientific explanations are <u>judged</u>
by <u>other scientists</u> who work in the <u>same field</u>.

2) Traditionally, new scientific explanations are announced
in <u>peer-reviewed journals</u>, or at <u>scientific conferences</u>.

3) Once other scientists have found out about a hypothesis
(through a journal or conference), they'll start to base
their <u>own predictions</u> on it and carry out their <u>own</u>
<u>experiments</u>. This allows them to <u>test</u> and <u>critically</u>
<u>evaluate</u> the new hypothesis.

4) When other scientists test the new hypothesis they will also try to <u>reproduce</u> the
earlier results. Results that <u>can't be reproduced</u> by another scientist <u>aren't</u> very <u>reliable</u>
(they're hard to trust) — and scientists tend to be pretty <u>sceptical</u> about them.

5) There's very little <u>confidence</u> in <u>new claims</u> that haven't been evaluated by
other scientists in this way.

A <u>peer-reviewed</u> journal is one where
<u>other scientists</u> check results and scientific
explanations <u>before</u> the journal is published.
They check that people have been '<u>scientific</u>'
about what they're saying (e.g. that
experiments have been done in a sensible
way). But this doesn't mean that the
findings are <u>correct</u>, just that they're not
wrong in any <u>obvious</u> kind of way.

If <u>Evidence</u> Supports a Hypothesis, It's <u>Accepted</u> — for Now

1) If a hypothesis <u>survives</u> the peer review process, then scientists start to
have a lot of <u>confidence</u> in it and accept it as a <u>theory</u>. Our currently accepted
theories have been tested many, many times over the years and survived.

2) Once scientists have gone through this process and
accepted a theory, they take a lot of <u>persuading</u>
to <u>drop it</u> — even if some <u>new data</u> appears that
<u>can't be explained</u> using the existing theory.

Some theories involve a model, which is a simplified
picture of what's going on with objects that can't be
observed directly. Other theories may talk about the
mathematical relationships between different quantities.

3) Until a <u>better</u>, more plausible explanation is found (one that can explain <u>both</u> the old
and new data), the <u>tried and tested</u> theory is likely to <u>stick around</u> — because it
already explains loads of <u>other observations</u> really well. And remember, scientists are
always <u>sceptical</u> about new data until it's been proved to be <u>reliable</u> (see above).

That's my theory and I'm sticking to it...

So there you have it. The scientific process in a <u>nutshell</u>. A two-page nutshell. More of a coconut shell really...
Never mind. The point is, these two pages contain <u>everything you need to know</u> about how scientists go from
making an observation, to coming up with a nice, neat explanation. And in case you were thinking this has no
relevance to you, you'll need to know it for your <u>controlled assessment</u> (see p. 77-80) and for your <u>exams</u>.

Data

This page is all about what scientists do with <u>data</u> and why it's so <u>important</u>...

Scientists Need <u>Reliable Data, Not Opinion,</u> to <u>Justify</u> an Explanation

1) The only <u>scientific</u> way to <u>test a hypothesis</u> is to gather <u>reliable data</u>.

2) Reliable data is data that has been <u>repeated</u> by a scientist lots of times or <u>reproduced</u> by other scientists in independent experiments.

3) <u>Opinions</u> are not <u>reliable data</u> — they can't be <u>reproduced</u> in an experiment by other scientists, so they can't be used to <u>support a hypothesis</u>.

Measurements Will <u>Always Vary</u> to Some Extent

1) If you take a lot of measurements of the <u>same thing</u>, you won't always get the <u>same result</u>.

2) This could be for lots of reasons, e.g. the <u>conditions</u> you're taking your measurements in change, or you've made a <u>mistake</u> when measuring (<u>human error</u>).

3) Because measurements of the same thing always vary, no <u>individual measurement</u> can be <u>relied upon</u> to give you the <u>true value</u> of the quantity you're measuring.

Repeating Measurements <u>Helps You to Estimate</u> the <u>True Value</u>

1) To get a <u>good estimate</u> of the true value, scientists must <u>repeat</u> their <u>measurements</u>.

2) Repeated measurements will have a <u>range</u> of values — some values will be <u>higher</u> than the true value and some will be <u>lower</u>. This means it's likely that the <u>true value</u> lies somewhere within this range.

3) The true value can then be <u>estimated</u> by <u>calculating</u> the <u>mean</u> (the average value — add up all the repeated results and divide by the total number of results).

4) Because individual results <u>vary</u>, the <u>mean</u> result is more likely to be close to the <u>true value</u>. This is because it accounts for the <u>variations</u> (both higher and lower) of <u>several repeats</u> — which should roughly <u>cancel each other out</u>.

5) Measurements that are obviously <u>outside</u> the range of repeated results are called <u>outliers</u> — they're usually a sign that something has gone <u>wrong</u>. If possible, a scientist will <u>check</u> the measurement — and if they've got a <u>good reason</u> to doubt its accuracy, they'll <u>ignore</u> it.

EXAMPLE: This table shows the results of an experiment to measure the <u>mass of a hamster</u> — the measurement was repeated 8 times:

1) The result of <u>test 3</u> is very <u>different</u> from the others. It's an <u>outlier</u>. It's likely that an error occurred when the measurement was taken, so it can be ignored.

2) The table suggests that the <u>true value</u> of the mass of the hamster is in the <u>range</u> of 191 – 195 g, where most of the measurements lie.

3) A <u>mean</u> (average) gives you the <u>best estimate</u> of the <u>true</u> value. In this case it works out at <u>193 g</u>.

Test	Mass of hamster (g)
1	193
2	194
3	128
4	191
5	193
6	192
7	195
8	192

<u>Working out averages — it's just mean...</u>

Data is the <u>cornerstone</u> of science — it's used to test <u>every</u> hypothesis, so it really is <u>pretty blummin' important</u>. What a shame then, that estimating the <u>true value</u> and spotting <u>outliers</u> isn't just a bit more fun... sigh...

Correlation and Cause

Correlation and cause come up a lot in science, so it's important that you understand the difference.

A Correlation is a Relationship Between Two Factors

1) Scientists often think about scientific processes as a load of different factors which might affect an outcome. For example, if the outcome is getting lung cancer, it might be affected by factors such as smoking, occupation, genes, etc.

2) They collect data and use it to look for relationships between a factor and an outcome.

3) If an outcome happens when a factor is there, but not when it isn't there, scientists say there's a correlation — i.e. the outcome is related to the factor.

4) If an outcome increases or decreases as a factor increases or decreases, they're also said to be correlated.

A Correlation Doesn't Prove One Thing Causes Another

Just because there's a correlation between a factor and an outcome, it doesn't mean that the factor causes the outcome. There might be another, hidden factor that's affecting them both. Here's an example:

> 1) Primary school children with bigger feet tend to be better at maths.
> There's a correlation between the factor (big feet) and the outcome (better maths skills).
> 2) But it'd be crazy to say that having big feet causes you to be better at maths
> (and even weirder to say that being good at maths causes bigger feet...).
> 3) There's another (hidden) factor involved — their age. Older children are usually better at maths.
> They also usually have bigger feet. Age affects both their maths skills and the size of their feet.

Sometimes a correlation is just when a factor makes an outcome more likely, but not inevitable. E.g. if you eat a diet high in saturated fat, it increases your risk of heart disease, but doesn't mean you will get it.

Scientists Need to Do Fair Tests

1) A scientist might notice a correlation between a factor and an outcome and hypothesise that the factor causes the outcome. To check this, they must then look for evidence by doing a scientific study.

2) To make their study a fair test, the scientist must control all the other factors that might influence the outcome. This will make sure that the only factor affecting the outcome is the one being studied (see page 77).

3) In a study, scientists can't usually test the whole population (e.g. all the organisms of a particular species) so they compare samples instead. A sample is just a portion of the population.

4) There are two ways that scientists can make sure their study is a fair test when comparing samples:

- The samples can be matched in every way apart from the factor that they're investigating.
- The samples can be chosen at random — then it's equally likely that all samples will be affected by other factors in the same way.

5) The larger the sample size used in a study, the more confident a scientist can be about their hypothesis. E.g. many people didn't have much confidence in the findings of a study linking the MMR vaccine to autism, because the sample size was too small — just 12 patients.

6) Scientists don't usually accept that a factor causes an outcome unless they can work out a plausible mechanism that links the two things. E.g. there's a higher rate of lung cancer in smokers than non-smokers — the factor (smoking) and the outcome (lung cancer) are correlated. Cigarette smoke contains cancer-causing chemicals and it's inhaled into the lungs — this is the mechanism.

All sheep die — Elvis died, so he must have been a sheep...

You read about correlations in the media all the time. Reporters often make the mistake of thinking that if two things are correlated then one must cause the other. However, you can't, can't, can't just think this. Got that?

Risk

By reading this page you are agreeing to the <u>risk</u> of a paper cut or severe drowsiness that could affect your ability to operate heavy machinery... Think carefully — the choice is yours.

Nothing is Completely Risk-Free

1) <u>Everything</u> that you do has a <u>risk</u> attached to it.

2) Some risks seem pretty <u>obvious</u>, or we've known about them for a while, like the risk of getting <u>heart disease</u> if you're overweight, or of having a <u>car accident</u> when you're travelling in a car.

3) <u>New technology</u> arising from <u>scientific advances</u> can bring <u>new risks</u>, e.g. some scientists believe that using a mobile phone a lot may be <u>harmful</u>.

4) You can estimate the <u>size</u> of a risk based on <u>how many times</u> something has happened in a big sample (e.g. 100 000 people) over a given <u>period</u> (say, a year). For example, you could assess the risk of a smoker developing lung cancer by recording how many people in a group of 100 000 smokers developed the disease in a one year period.

5) To make a <u>decision</u> about an activity that involves a <u>risk</u>, we need to take into account the <u>chance</u> of the risk happening and how <u>serious</u> the <u>consequences</u> would be if it did. So if an activity involves a risk that's <u>very likely</u> to happen, with <u>serious consequences</u> if it does, that activity is considered <u>high risk</u>.

People Make Their Own Decisions About Risk

1) Not all risks have the same <u>consequences</u>, e.g. if you chop veg with a sharp knife you risk cutting your finger, but if you go scuba-diving you risk death. You're much <u>more likely</u> to cut your finger during half an hour of <u>chopping</u> than to die during half an hour of <u>scuba-diving</u>. But most people are happier to accept a higher <u>probability</u> of an accident if the <u>consequences</u> are <u>short-lived</u> and fairly <u>minor</u>.

2) People also tend to be more willing to accept a risk if they're <u>choosing</u> to do something (e.g. go scuba diving), rather than if they're having the risk <u>imposed</u> on them (e.g. being in a public place where <u>other people</u> are smoking).

3) People's <u>perception</u> of risk (how risky they <u>think</u> something is) isn't always <u>accurate</u>. They tend to view <u>familiar</u> activities as <u>low-risk</u> and <u>unfamiliar</u> activities as <u>high-risk</u> — even if that's not the case. For example, cycling on roads is often <u>high-risk</u>, but many people are happy to do it because it's a <u>familiar</u> activity. Air travel is actually pretty <u>safe</u>, but a lot of people perceive it as <u>high-risk</u>.

4) People also tend to <u>over-estimate</u> the risk of things whose effect lasts a <u>long time</u>, or is <u>invisible</u>, e.g. ionising radiation.

We have to Choose Acceptable Levels of Risk

1) Activities have different <u>benefits</u> and <u>risks</u> for <u>different groups of people</u>. For example, in building and running a <u>new nuclear power station</u>:

- <u>Construction companies</u> benefit from years of work in building the power station.
- <u>Local people</u> benefit from new jobs — but risk suffering from higher radiation exposure.
- The <u>national population</u> benefits from a reliable source of electricity — but some people may be at risk.
- There's a <u>global</u> benefit because nuclear power contributes a lot less to climate change than burning fossil fuels — but there's a global risk too, from a major accident like the Chernobyl disaster.

2) To make a <u>decision</u> about a course of action (e.g. whether or not to build a new nuclear power station) we need to <u>weigh up</u> the benefits and risks involved for everyone.

3) <u>Governments</u> and <u>public bodies</u> are often the ones who have to choose on behalf of <u>other people</u> whether the <u>risks</u> for a particular course of action are <u>acceptable</u>. Sometimes their decisions can be <u>controversial</u>, especially if the people who are <u>most at risk</u> are <u>not</u> the ones that <u>benefit</u>.

Not revising — an unacceptable exam risk...

All activities pose some sort of risk, it's just a question of deciding whether that risk is <u>worth it</u> in the long run.

Science — Benefits and Costs

Science can give us amazing things — cures for diseases, space travel, heated toilet seats...
But sometimes, these things come at a cost.

Scientific Technology Usually Has Benefits and Costs

Scientists have created loads of new technologies that could improve our lives.
In genetics, for example, benefits include:

1) Being able to identify whether a fetus has a genetic disorder.
2) Identifying whether an adult is likely to get a disease, such as cancer, later in life.
3) Growth of human (or animal) cells to be used as spare parts, for example in transplant surgery.
4) The possibility of being able to cure some genetic disorders.
5) Genetically engineering plants with useful characteristics, e.g. insect resistance in crops.

However, it's not all good news. Sometimes new technology can have unintended
or undesired impacts on our quality of life or the environment. For example:

1) Altering someone's genes to cure a genetic disorder might affect their health in other ways
   — there's no way of knowing in advance. This could reduce their overall quality of life.
2) Genetically engineered plants might have negative effects on the environment —
   it's possible that they could out-compete native plants, causing them to die out.

When developing new technologies, the benefits should always be weighed against the costs.

Human Activities Impact on the Environment

1) Even when we don't mean to, human beings have a huge effect on our surroundings. Science
   can help us to identify some of the unintentional impacts our activities have on the environment.
   For example, the main impacts of massive human population growth are:

   • We're using more land — we need land to build houses, grow crops and farm animals.
     To get it we often have to cut down forests and take over grassland.
   • We're using more non-renewable resources — these are resources (such as fuels)
     that will eventually run out, e.g. oil, coal and natural gas.
   • We're polluting more — more people means more rubbish, sewage, cars and industry,
     which can seriously damage the environment.

2) Scientists can also help us to minimise the effects of our activities and make the
   way we live more sustainable — i.e. less damaging to the environment, so that we
   don't use up resources for future generations (see page 38). For example:

   • Developing techniques for improving crop yield should mean we can grow more
     crops in a smaller area — so less land gets taken up by agriculture.
   • Developing technology which generates electricity from renewable energy
     sources (e.g. wind power, solar power) should help reduce the need for us to
     use coal, oil and natural gas as fuels — so they'll last longer.

Revision benefits include passing your exams...

The car is a good example of an advance in scientific technology that has improved our quality of life, but had
an unintentional negative impact on the environment. Science is now helping us to reduce this negative effect
though, by developing cleaner and more renewable energy sources for cars to run on. Excellent.

Science and Ethics

Science can often raise <u>important</u> issues to do with <u>ethics</u> — whether something is morally <u>right</u> or <u>wrong</u>...

Some Questions Are <u>Unanswerable</u> by Science

1) There are some questions that all the experiments in the world <u>won't</u> help us answer — the "<u>Should we be doing this at all?</u>" type questions.

2) Take <u>embryo screening</u> (which allows you to choose an embryo with particular characteristics). It's <u>possible</u> to do it — but does that mean we <u>should</u>?

3) Different people have <u>different opinions</u>. For example...

> Some people say it's <u>good</u>... couples whose <u>existing</u> child needs a <u>bone marrow transplant</u>, but who can't find a donor, will be able to have <u>another</u> child selected for its <u>matching</u> bone marrow. This would <u>save</u> the life of their first child — and if they <u>want</u> another child anyway... where's the harm?
>
> Other people say it's <u>bad</u>... they say it could have serious effects on the <u>new child</u>. In the above example the new child might feel <u>unwanted</u> — thinking they were only brought into the world to help <u>someone else</u>. And would they have the right to <u>refuse</u> to donate their bone marrow (as anyone else would)?

4) This question of whether something is <u>morally</u> right or wrong <u>can't be answered</u> by more <u>experiments</u> — there is <u>no "right" or "wrong"</u> answer.

5) The best we can do is get a <u>consensus</u> from society — a <u>judgement</u> that <u>most people</u> are more or less happy to live by. <u>Science</u> can provide <u>more information</u> to help people make this judgement, and the judgement might <u>change</u> over time. But in the end it's up to <u>people</u> and their <u>conscience</u>.

There Are <u>Two</u> Key Arguments About <u>Ethical Dilemmas</u>

1 Some people think that certain actions are <u>always unnatural</u> or <u>wrong</u>. This means that, whatever the possible benefits, they feel these actions are <u>unacceptable</u>. Some people would say that research on human embryos comes into this category.

2 Some people may say that the <u>right decision</u> is the one that brings the <u>greatest benefit</u> to the <u>greatest number</u> of people. These people might argue that embryo research does <u>more good</u> than harm and so it is acceptable.

The <u>Law</u> is Sometimes Involved Too

The <u>law</u> is involved in regulating some areas of scientific research, for example:

1) <u>Animal research</u> is regulated. For example, in the UK, scientists researching on <u>vertebrates</u> must have a licence and they must show that the likely <u>benefits</u> of the research <u>outweigh</u> any animal suffering.

2) <u>Genetic manipulation</u> is also regulated. In Britain, genetic manipulation of human body cells is allowed, but the modification of <u>reproductive cells</u> (sperm and egg cells) isn't.

3) There are regulations about the effect of research on the <u>environment</u>, e.g. <u>pollution</u> is monitored.

4) All sites carrying out <u>nuclear research</u> have to abide by strict <u>health and safety laws</u>.

Hmmm, tricky...

As you can see, science isn't just about knowing your <u>facts</u>. You need to think about the <u>ethical issues</u> of new technology — as well as the kinds of <u>arguments</u> people consider to make decisions about what should be done.

Genes, Chromosomes and DNA

Welcome to the first Biology bit of the OCR 21st Century Science Revision Guide. You're gonna love it.

1) Most cells in your body have a nucleus — and it's the nucleus that contains your genetic material.

2) The genetic material in the nucleus is arranged into chromosomes. The human cell nucleus contains 23 pairs of chromosomes.

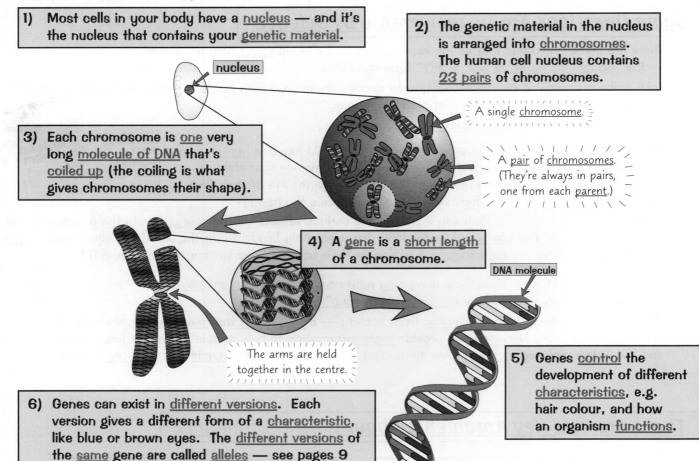

nucleus

A single chromosome.

3) Each chromosome is one very long molecule of DNA that's coiled up (the coiling is what gives chromosomes their shape).

A pair of chromosomes. (They're always in pairs, one from each parent.)

4) A gene is a short length of a chromosome.

DNA molecule

The arms are held together in the centre.

5) Genes control the development of different characteristics, e.g. hair colour, and how an organism functions.

6) Genes can exist in different versions. Each version gives a different form of a characteristic, like blue or brown eyes. The different versions of the same gene are called alleles — see pages 9 and 10 for more information.

Genes are Instructions for Cells

Each gene is a code for making a certain protein. Proteins are the building blocks of cells. Having different versions of proteins means that we end up with different characteristics.

1) Some proteins are structural proteins. They're part of things like skin, hair, blood, and the cytoplasm in our cells. E.g. collagen is a structural protein that is found in tendons, bones and cartilage.

2) Other proteins are functional proteins. For example, enzymes are proteins that help with digestion by breaking down food molecules — amylase is a digestive enzyme that breaks down starch to maltose.

An Organism's Genotype Describes the Genes It's Got

1) An organism's genotype is all of the genes it has. The characteristics that an organism displays are called its phenotype.

2) Some characteristics, e.g. dimples, are controlled only by genes. This can just be one gene, or quite often the characteristic is controlled by several genes working together, e.g. eye colour.

3) Other characteristics, e.g. scars, are controlled only by environmental factors. They don't have anything to do with genes and are caused by things like how and where you live.

4) There are also characteristics that are controlled by both genes and environmental factors. For example, weight — if both your parents are skinny, you'll probably be skinny. But not if all you eat are donuts.

It's hard being a DNA molecule, there's so much to remember...

You need to understand everything on this page — it'll help everything else to make sense later on. To see how much of it you can remember, cover the page, scribble down the main points and then learn the bits you missed.

Genes and Variation

Thought the fact that you haven't got your dad's <u>horrendous bushy eyebrows</u> was just a happy coincidence? Well, there's a bit more to it...

Sperm and Egg Cells Have Half the Normal Amount of DNA

In body cells (all your cells apart from sex cells), <u>chromosomes</u> come in <u>pairs</u> (because we have <u>two parents</u>). One chromosome in every pair has come from each parent.

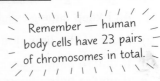

Remember — human body cells have 23 pairs of chromosomes in total.

1) The <u>sex cells</u> (the sperm and the egg) are different from ordinary body cells because they contain just <u>23 single chromosomes</u> — that's one chromosome from each pair.

2) When the sperm <u>fertilises</u> the egg (during <u>sexual reproduction</u>), the 23 chromosomes in the sperm combine with the 23 chromosomes in the egg.

3) The fertilised egg then has 23 <u>pairs</u> of chromosomes, just like an ordinary body cell.

4) The two chromosomes in a pair always carry the <u>same genes</u> and each gene is always found in the <u>same place</u> on the two chromosomes. Because the two chromosomes in a pair came from different parents, they might have different alleles of these genes. <u>Alleles</u> are different <u>versions</u> of the same gene.

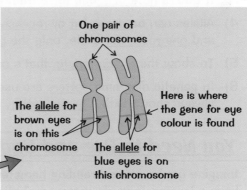

One pair of chromosomes

The <u>allele</u> for brown eyes is on this chromosome

Here is where the gene for eye colour is found

The <u>allele</u> for blue eyes is on this chromosome

Children Resemble Both Parents, But Are Identical to Neither

So, <u>half</u> a child's chromosomes have come from <u>each parent</u>. This means that:

1) Children get <u>some</u> of their alleles from <u>each</u> of their parents.

2) This is why most children look a bit like <u>both</u> of their parents.

3) But they won't be <u>exactly</u> like either one of their parents because they haven't got <u>all</u> the same alleles — some came from the <u>other</u> parent.

4) In fact, every child will have a new, <u>unique</u>, combination of alleles — that's why no two people in the world are exactly the same (apart from identical twins, but you don't need to worry about that 'til page 14).

Genes Are Shuffled Together Randomly to Make Eggs and Sperm

When people <u>produce sperm</u> or <u>egg</u> cells, their pairs of chromosomes <u>separate</u> and go into different cells.

1) The two chromosomes in a pair are <u>never identical</u> because they have <u>different alleles</u>.

2) So, when they go into two different sex cells, each of the two cells gets <u>different alleles</u>.

3) Each of the 23 chromosome pairs separates <u>independently</u>.

4) So there are <u>millions</u> of different <u>chromosome combinations</u> that can be produced from the separation of 23 pairs. (Actually, about 8 million different combinations.)

5) This means that all the <u>sex cells</u> produced by one individual will probably all be <u>genetically different</u>.

6) When a woman releases an egg it can be fertilised by <u>any one</u> of millions of different sperm released by her partner.

7) All of this means that the chances of two siblings being identical are <u>absolutely minuscule</u>. Brothers and sisters tend to look a bit alike, but there are <u>always differences</u>.

Genes — they always come in pairs...

So, a mixture of chromosomes are <u>randomly shuffled</u> up as they go into the sex cells. Then a random sex cell fuses with another <u>random</u> sex cell at <u>fertilisation</u> (oh, the romance of it all).

Inheritance and Genetic Diagrams

Genetic diagrams are really handy for working out how characteristics move from one generation to the next.

The Combination of Alleles Determines the Phenotype

When you've got two copies of a gene, usually only one of them can be expressed in the phenotype:

1) As I keep saying, alleles are different versions of the same gene.

2) Most of the time you have two of each gene (i.e. two alleles) — one from each parent.

3) If you're homozygous for a trait, you have two alleles the same for that particular gene.
   If you're heterozygous for a trait, you have two different alleles for that particular gene.

4) Alleles can be dominant or recessive. If you have two dominant alleles for a gene or one dominant and one recessive allele, only the characteristic that's caused by the dominant allele will be shown.

5) To show the characteristic that's caused by the recessive allele, both alleles for a gene have to be recessive.

6) In genetic diagrams, letters are used to represent alleles. Alleles that produce dominant characteristics are always shown with a capital letter, and alleles that produce recessive characteristics with a small letter.

You Need to Use and Understand Genetic Diagrams

Imagine you're cross-breeding hamsters, and that some have a normal, boring disposition while others have a leaning towards crazy acrobatics. And suppose you know the behaviour is due to one gene...

Let's say that the allele which causes the crazy nature is recessive — so use a 'b'.
And normal (boring) behaviour is due to a dominant allele — call it 'B'.

1) A crazy hamster must have the alleles 'bb' (i.e. it must be homozygous for this trait).

2) However, a normal hamster could be BB (homozygous) or Bb (heterozygous), because the dominant allele (B) overrules the recessive one (b).

3) The genetic diagram below shows what could happen when two normal hamsters (Bb) are crossed:

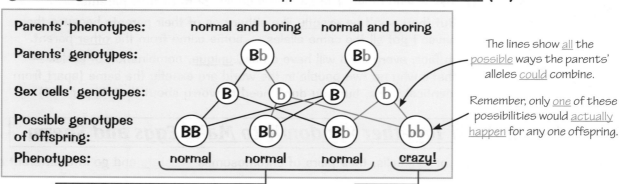

Parents' phenotypes:	normal and boring	normal and boring
Parents' genotypes:	Bb	Bb
Sex cells' genotypes:	B b	B b
Possible genotypes of offspring:	BB Bb	Bb bb
Phenotypes:	normal normal	normal crazy!

The lines show all the possible ways the parents' alleles could combine.

Remember, only one of these possibilities would actually happen for any one offspring.

There's a 75% chance of having a normal hamster, and a 25% chance of a crazy one.

4) Knowing how inheritance works can help you to interpret a family tree.

5) The case of the new hamster in the family tree is just the same as in the genetic diagram above.

6) Both of its parents have the alleles Bb — so there's a 75% chance the hamster could be normal (BB or Bb) and a 25% chance that it'll be crazy (bb).

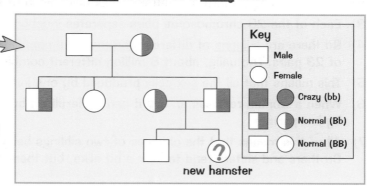

Key
- Male
- Female
- Crazy (bb)
- Normal (Bb)
- Normal (BB)

new hamster

It's not just hamsters that have the crazy allele...

... my sister has it too. Remember, 'results' like this are only probabilities. It doesn't mean it'll actually happen.

Genetic Diagrams and Sex Chromosomes

Just when you thought you'd finished with genetic diagrams these things called Punnett squares march into view. Oh well, at least you can cheer yourself up by also finding out exactly why you are a boy or a girl.

Punnett Squares are Another Type of Genetic Diagram

Another way of working out a genetic cross is by using Punnett squares.
They are basically just grids — so don't panic.

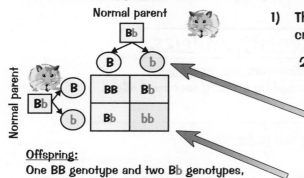

Normal parent

Bb

Normal parent

Bb

	B	b
B	BB	Bb
b	Bb	bb

Offspring:
One BB genotype and two Bb genotypes,
so there's a 75% chance of having a
normal, boring hamster. One bb genotype,
so there's a 25% chance of having
a crazy hamster.

1) The diagram on the left shows how you would draw the hamster cross from the previous page using a Punnett square.

2) The first bit's the same as a normal genetic diagram — you work out what alleles the sex cells would have from the parents' genotypes.

3) Then you just write the sex cells' alleles (from one parent) along the left-hand side of the square, and along the top of the square (from the other parent).

4) Then you pair them up in the boxes to see the different possible combinations of alleles in the offspring.

Your Chromosomes Control Whether You're Male or Female

There are 23 pairs of chromosomes in every human body cell. The 23rd pair are labelled XY. These are sex chromosomes — they decide whether you turn out male or female.

> All men have an X and a Y chromosome: **XY**
> The Y chromosome causes male characteristics.
>
> All women have two X chromosomes: **XX**
> The lack of a Y chromosome causes female characteristics.

female parent

XX

male parent

XY

	X	X
X	XX	XX
Y	XY	XY

Offspring:
Two XX genotypes and
two XY genotypes, so
there's a 50% chance
of having either a girl
or a boy.

Like all other characteristics, sex is determined by a gene. The Y chromosome carries a gene which makes an embryo develop into a male as it grows. Females, who always have two X chromosomes, don't have this gene and so they develop in a different way.

The genetic diagram for sex inheritance is fairly similar to a bog-standard one. It just shows the sex chromosomes rather than different alleles.

One Gene Determines Which Sex Organs You Develop

1) The gene that makes an embryo into a male causes a specific protein to be produced.

2) When the embryo's reproductive system begins to develop, this protein causes the development of testes (instead of ovaries).

3) The testes then produce male sex hormones, which in turn make the rest of the male reproductive system develop.

4) In females the protein is not produced, so the embryo develops ovaries and the rest of a female reproductive system.

I thought it was all to do with crisps and cereal...

I have a theory that the two big differences between boys and girls are that boys eat crisps more than one at a time and they mix different types of cereal together in the same bowl. It's just a theory though.

Genetic Disorders

The alleles of some genes can be __faulty__ which can cause some pretty __nasty__ disorders.
Since the disorders are a genetic problem, they can be __passed on__ from parents to children.

Genetic Disorders __Are Caused by__ Faulty Alleles

1) Some __disorders__ are __inherited__ — one or both parents carry a __faulty allele__ and pass it on to their children.
2) __Cystic fibrosis__ and __Huntington's disease__ are both caused by a faulty allele of a __single gene__.

Some Genetic Disorders __Are Caused by__ Recessive Alleles...

Most of the __defective alleles__ that are responsible for genetic disorders are __recessive__.
__Cystic fibrosis__ is a __genetic disorder__ of the __cell membranes__ caused by a faulty recessive allele.
It __results__ in some pretty nasty symptoms:

- __Thick sticky mucus__ in the __air passages__, __gut__ and __pancreas__.
- __Breathing difficulty__.
- __Chest infections__ (lots of painful coughing).
- __Difficulty in digesting food__ (sufferers are often short and skinny as a result).

1) The allele which causes cystic fibrosis is a __recessive allele__, 'f', carried by about __1 person in 25__.
2) Because it's recessive, people with only __one copy__ of the allele __won't__ show the symptoms of the disorder — they're known as __carriers__.
3) For a child to have a chance of inheriting the disorder, __both parents__ must be __carriers__ or __sufferers__.
4) As the diagram shows, there's a __1 in 4 chance__ of a child having the disorder if __both__ parents are __carriers__.

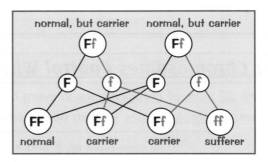

...Others Are Caused by Dominant Alleles

Remember that Punnett squares are just another way of drawing genetic diagrams (see page 11).

Carrier/sufferer parent

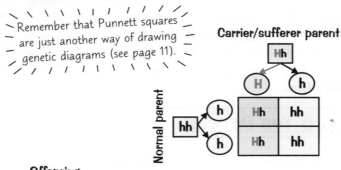

Offspring
Two Hh genotypes so 50% of the offspring will be carriers/sufferers. Two hh genotypes so the other 50% of the offspring will be normal.

So, if one parent is a sufferer, there's a 50% chance of each of their children having the disorder.

1) Unlike cystic fibrosis, __Huntington's disease__ is caused by a __dominant__ allele.
2) The disorder causes __tremors__ (shaking), __clumsiness__, __memory loss__, __mood changes__ and __poor concentration__. There's __no cure__.
3) The dominant allele means there's a __50%__ chance of each child inheriting the disorder if just one parent is a carrier. These are __seriously grim__ odds.
4) The "carrier" parent will of course be a __sufferer__ too since the allele is __dominant__, but the disease has a __late onset__ — the symptoms do not usually appear until after the age of 40, by which time the allele has been __passed on__ to children and even grandchildren. Hence the disorder persists.

Unintentional mooning — caused by faulty genes...
We __all__ have defective genes in us somewhere — but usually they don't cause us a problem (as they're often __recessive__, so if you have a healthy __dominant__ allele too, you'll be fine). At the moment scientists are looking at new ways of treating genetic disorders, but it'll be a while until these diseases are a thing of the past.

Genetic Testing

Nowadays it's possible to <u>test</u> for all sorts of different genetic conditions, but this has thrown up some pretty big <u>issues</u>.

Genetic Testing can be Used On Embryos, Children and Adults

1) When <u>embryos</u> are produced using <u>IVF</u> (*in vitro* fertilisation), doctors can <u>test</u> the embryos to check if they've got certain genetic disorders. This is known as <u>pre-implantation genetic diagnosis</u> and is especially important if there's concern that one of the parents might carry alleles for a genetic disorder. When the embryos are tested, only <u>healthy</u> ones are chosen to be <u>implanted</u> into the mother's <u>womb</u> — embryos with a genetic disorder are <u>discarded</u>.

2) <u>Children</u> and <u>adults</u> can be checked to see if they <u>carry alleles</u> for genetic disorders. For example, couples might do this to find out if their children are <u>likely to inherit</u> a particular genetic disorder.

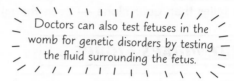
Doctors can also test fetuses in the womb for genetic disorders by testing the fluid surrounding the fetus.

3) <u>Children</u> and <u>adults</u> can also be tested <u>before</u> certain <u>drugs</u> are prescribed to them. This can show how a drug is likely to <u>affect</u> an individual, e.g. if the drug will be an <u>effective treatment</u>, or if the person will have an <u>adverse reaction</u> to it.

There are Issues Surrounding Genetic Testing

<u>Having these tests</u> then getting the results from them causes all sorts of <u>issues</u>:

1) The results of genetic tests may not be 100% <u>accurate</u>. There are often <u>errors</u> due to things like samples getting <u>contaminated</u> or <u>misinterpretation</u> of results. This means that healthy people could be told that they have a genetic disorder (a <u>false positive</u> result) or people with a disorder could be told that they are fit and well (a <u>false negative</u> result). Because of this, people might make decisions based on <u>incorrect</u> information.

2) Like most medical procedures, tests carried out during pregnancy aren't 100% <u>safe</u>, e.g. doing a genetic test on the fluid around a fetus causes a <u>miscarriage</u> in 0.5 to 1% of cases.

3) If a test result is <u>positive</u>, should other members of a family be <u>tested</u>? Some people may prefer not to know, but is this <u>fair</u> on any partners or future children they might have?

4) Is it <u>right</u> for someone who's at risk of passing on a genetic condition to have <u>children</u>? Is it <u>fair</u> to put them under pressure <u>not to</u>, if they decide they want children?

5) If a test carried out during a pregnancy is positive, is it right to <u>terminate</u> the pregnancy? Perhaps the parents wouldn't be able to <u>cope</u> with a sick or disabled child, but does that child have less <u>right to life</u> than a healthy child? Some people think abortion is <u>always wrong</u>, whatever the circumstances.

6) If the results become available to others, this might cause <u>discrimination</u>. <u>Employers</u> might not want to give a job to someone who is likely to get ill. However, some people argue that employers might be able to use the results of genetic tests to make sure that they don't <u>expose</u> their employees to anything that might be especially <u>dangerous</u> to them because of the genes they have.

7) <u>Insurance companies</u> might refuse to give <u>life insurance</u> to people with the "wrong" alleles.

Get ready for some genetic testing in the exam...

You need to understand <u>what</u> genetic testing is used for, and you also need to get to grips with the altogether more prickly <u>issues</u> that genetic testing raises. There are a lot of words on here I know, but trust me, they can't hurt you. In fact, they can only make your exam grades more healthy, so read them over a couple of times.

Clones

Cloning always seems to be a hot topic in the news, but nature has been making clones for millions of years and nobody seems that bothered.

Clones Are Genetically Identical Organisms

1) Sexual reproduction produces offspring that are genetically different. But bacteria, some plants and some animals can reproduce asexually (without sexual reproduction) to form clones.

2) Clones are genetically identical organisms — they have the same genes, and the same alleles of those genes.

3) Because clones have the same alleles, any differences between them must be due to differences in their environment — for example, if you were better nourished than your clone as a child, you would probably be taller than your clone — even though your alleles would still be identical.

Nature Makes Clones...

(i) By Asexual Reproduction

Asexual reproduction means that there is only one parent, and the offspring are genetically identical to each other and the parent.

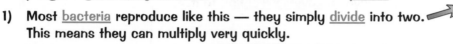

1) Most bacteria reproduce like this — they simply divide into two. This means they can multiply very quickly.

2) Many plants can also reproduce asexually:

- Some plants produce horizontal stems called runners that move out from the base of the plant and form new clones at their tips, e.g. strawberry plants.

- Other plants produce underground fleshy structures called bulbs. These can then grow to form a new identical plant, e.g. garlic.

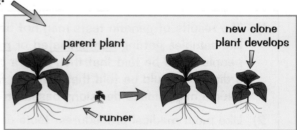

3) A few animals can reproduce asexually. Female greenfly don't need to mate — they can just lay eggs, which develop into more identical females. They can also reproduce sexually, when they feel like it.

(ii) When Cells of an Embryo Split

Identical twins are also clones.

1) A single egg is fertilised by a sperm, and an embryo begins to develop as normal.

2) Occasionally, the embryo splits into two, and two separate embryos begin to develop.

3) The two embryos are genetically identical. So, two genetically identical babies are born.

Scientists Can Now Make Animal Clones in the Lab

1) The nucleus of an egg cell is removed — this leaves the egg cell without any genetic information.

2) A nucleus from an adult donor cell is inserted in its place.

3) The cell is then stimulated so that it starts dividing as if it was a normal embryo (fertilised egg).

4) The embryo produced is genetically identical to the donor cell.

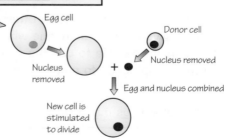

An evil dictator might make an army of clones to rule the Galaxy...

That might be a good idea for a film, come to think of it. Make sure you know the ways that clones are produced naturally and the way they can be produced artificially by scientists. So, learn everything on the page, cover it up and see if you can clone it onto a blank piece of paper.

Stem Cells

Stem cell research has <u>exciting possibilities</u> but some of the research is still in its <u>early stages</u>.

Stem Cells Can Become Other Types of Cells

1) Most cells in your body are <u>specialised</u> for a particular job. E.g. white blood cells are brilliant at fighting invaders, but they can't carry oxygen like red blood cells.

2) Most cells in multicellular organisms become <u>specialised</u> during the <u>early development</u> of the organism.

3) Some cells are <u>unspecialised</u>. They can develop into <u>different types of cells</u> depending on what <u>instructions</u> they're given. These cells are called <u>STEM CELLS</u>.

4) There are <u>two main types</u> of stem cell:

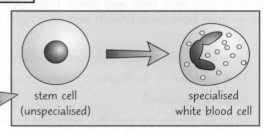
stem cell (unspecialised) → specialised white blood cell

Some people <u>object</u> to stem cell research and treatments. They say it is <u>unethical</u> to take cells from an embryo and that using stem cells is '<u>playing God</u>'.

1) Embryonic Stem Cells

• These are <u>unspecialised</u> cells found in early <u>embryos</u>.

• The stem cells are <u>removed</u> from the embryo, then the embryo is <u>destroyed</u>.

• They're <u>exciting</u> to doctors and medical researchers because they have the potential to turn into <u>ANY</u> kind of cell at all.

• This makes sense if you think about it — <u>all</u> the <u>different types</u> of cell found in an organism have to come from those <u>few cells</u> in the early embryo.

Our scientists believe they have found a potentially limitless supply of stem cells...

2) Adult Stem Cells

• These are <u>unspecialised</u> cells that can be found in <u>adult</u> animals.

• They're involved in <u>maintaining and repairing</u> old and damaged <u>tissues</u> and can specialise into <u>many</u> cell types (but <u>not all</u> cell types).

• These stem cells can be <u>safely removed</u> from adult patients, e.g. by extracting their bone marrow — <u>no embryos</u> have to be <u>destroyed</u>.

Stem Cells May Be Used to Treat Many Illnesses

1) Medicine <u>already</u> uses <u>adult stem cells</u> to cure disease. For example, people with some <u>blood diseases</u> (e.g. <u>sickle cell anaemia</u>) can be treated by <u>bone marrow transplants</u>. Bone marrow contains <u>adult stem cells</u> that can turn into <u>new blood cells</u> to replace the faulty old ones.

2) Embryonic stem cells could also be used to <u>replace</u> faulty cells in sick people — you could make beating <u>heart muscle cells</u> for people with heart disease, <u>insulin-producing cells</u> for people with <u>diabetes</u>, <u>nerve cells</u> for people <u>paralysed by spinal injuries</u>, and so on. These embryonic stem cell treatments are <u>still being researched</u> though, so they might not be available for a while yet.

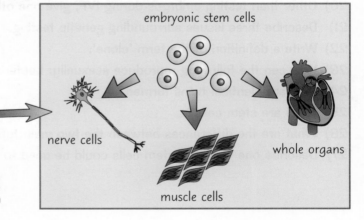
embryonic stem cells → nerve cells, muscle cells, whole organs

Embryonic stem cells — the original Jack of all trades...

Another exciting prospect is making an <u>embryo</u> that's a <u>clone</u> of a patient with an illness. Stem cells could then be extracted from the embryo — the big advantage is that the body <u>wouldn't reject</u> them.

Revision Summary for Module B1

Well, who'd have thought it? A conveniently-placed list of revision questions just for you. Granted, it's not the most fun you're ever going to have, but doing these questions is a really useful way of seeing which topics you're comfortable with and which ones you need to brush up on. There's no time like the present, so here goes — just hold your breath and dive right in...

1) Where are chromosomes found within a cell?

2) True or false — in humans, chromosomes are usually found in groups of four?

3) What are alleles?

4) How do genes control the different characteristics we develop?

5) What do the words 'genotype' and 'phenotype' mean?

6) Is a person's weight determined by genes, the environment or a combination of both?

7) Name the two types of sex cell.

8) How many chromosomes are found in sex cells?

9) Why do most children look a bit like both of their parents but not identical to either?

10) What's the difference between homozygous and heterozygous?

11)* Draw a genetic diagram for the possible inheritance of an allele for loving Aston Villa (the football club). The allele is dominant and one parent is homozygous (AA) and one is heterozygous (Aa).

12)* Now draw a Punnett square diagram for the inheritance of the same allele where one parent is homozygous (aa) and one is heterozygous (Aa).

13) What sex chromosomes do human males have?

14) How does a gene on one of the human sex chromosomes cause embryos to develop into males?

15) Is the allele for cystic fibrosis dominant or recessive?

16) What are the symptoms of cystic fibrosis?

17) What are the symptoms of Huntington's disease?

18) What is the chance of a child inheriting Huntington's disease if one of their parents has one copy of the faulty allele?

19) During IVF treatment, what is the process of testing embryos to see if they have a genetic disorder called?

20) Other than testing embryos during IVF, give one other use of genetic testing.

21) Describe three issues surrounding genetic testing.

22) Write a definition of the term 'clone'.

23) How can the following reproduce asexually: bacteria, some plants and some animals?

24) How are identical twins formed?

25) What are stem cells?

26) What are the differences between the two main types of stem cells?

27) Describe one way that stem cells could be used to treat an illness.

* Answers on page 84.

Microorganisms and Disease

Microorganisms include things like <u>bacteria</u>, <u>viruses</u> and some <u>fungi</u>. Some of them cause <u>infectious diseases</u>.

Symptoms *Can Be Caused by Cell Damage or by Toxins*

1) The effects that an infection has on the body, such as a <u>fever</u> (raised body temperature) or a <u>rash</u>, are called the <u>symptoms</u>. Different microorganisms cause different symptoms, but they all damage the body in one way or another. The damage is done to the body's <u>cells</u>.

2) Some microorganisms damage cells <u>directly</u>. For example, <u>malaria</u> parasites invade red blood cells and multiply inside them, eventually making the cells burst open. Malaria causes <u>flu-like</u> symptoms.

3) Many infectious microorganisms produce <u>poisons</u> (<u>toxins</u>) that damage cells:

   • Some bacteria produce <u>proteins</u> that damage the material holding cells together. This helps the bacteria to <u>invade</u> the body more deeply, e.g. *Staphylococcus* bacteria can cause food poisoning.

   • Other microorganisms produce toxins that <u>poison</u> cells, causing <u>fever</u> or <u>inflammation</u> (painful swelling). Some strains of *Escherichia coli* cause <u>diarrhoea</u> by secreting toxic substances.

Microorganisms *Reproduce Quickly Inside the Human Body*

1) <u>Bacteria</u> reproduce by making copies of themselves. To do this they need a source of <u>nutrients</u> for energy, and they need <u>warm</u>, <u>moist</u> conditions so the chemical reactions inside them can take place.

2) Unfortunately for us, there are lots of places <u>inside</u> the <u>human body</u> where you find these conditions (e.g. in your intestines), so a few bacteria can quickly become a <u>large colony</u> inside the body.

3) Viruses need <u>other cells</u> to reproduce — they use parts of the other cells make copies of themselves.

4) Certain viruses can <u>easily reproduce</u> inside the human body as there are lots of the right kind of cells for them to use.

You can *Calculate the Growth of a Microorganism Population*

1) Microorganisms <u>reproduce</u> by making a <u>copy</u> of themselves. The <u>copies</u>, and the <u>original</u> microorganisms, can then go on to reproduce and make <u>more copies</u>.

2) So, if you start with <u>one</u> microorganism that reproduces in <u>30 minutes</u>, after that time you'll have <u>two</u> microorganisms. After <u>60 minutes</u>, you'll have <u>four</u> microorganisms and after <u>90 minutes</u>, you'll have <u>eight</u> microorganisms...

3) ... You probably get the idea — after each reproduction period, there'll be <u>twice as many</u> microorganisms as there were at the end of the previous reproduction period.

4) To <u>work out</u> the <u>size</u> of a microorganism population after a certain amount of time, you need to know:

   • The <u>number</u> of microorganisms before reproduction starts.

   • How <u>long</u> it takes for one microorganism to <u>reproduce</u>. ◄—— These two should be in the same unit of time, e.g. minutes or hours.

   • How <u>long</u> the microorganisms are <u>left</u> to reproduce for. ◄——

Here's a <u>worked</u> example:

Revisium biologus is a bacterium that reproduces once every <u>20 minutes</u> at 38 °C. If <u>10 *R. biologus* bacteria</u> are left to reproduce for <u>2 hours</u>, how many bacteria will there be at the end of this period?

1) 2 hours = <u>120 minutes</u>. For *R. biologus* this is 120 ÷ 20 = <u>6 reproduction periods</u>.

2) To work out the number of bacteria after the <u>first reproduction period</u>, all you need to do is <u>multiply</u> the number of bacteria you started with <u>by 2</u>: 10 x 2 = 20

3) Then work out the number you'd have after the <u>second reproduction period</u>: 20 x 2 = 40

4) Keep going until you've done all <u>six</u> reproduction periods.
   Your answer should be that after 2 hours, you'd end up with <u>640</u> *R. biologus* bacteria.

Don't get put off — microorganisms really grow on you...

Microorganism populations can <u>grow</u> surprisingly <u>quickly</u>. If you're talking about microorganisms that cause <u>horrible diseases</u>, it's not great — the <u>more microorganisms</u> there are, the <u>more damage</u> they can do.

The Immune System

From time to time microorganisms <u>do</u> make it into the body. But all is not lost, as your body has a pretty powerful <u>weapon</u> to deal with them — your <u>white blood cells</u>.

<u>Your</u> Immune System <u>Fights Off</u> Invading Microbes

The role of the <u>immune system</u> is to deal with any infectious microorganisms that enter the body. An immune response <u>always</u> involves <u>white blood cells</u>. There are several <u>different types</u> and they all have different jobs to do.

All white blood cells are part of the immune system.

1) Anything that gets into the body should be picked up straight away by a certain type of white blood cell.

2) These white blood cells are able to detect things that are '<u>foreign</u>' to the body, e.g. microorganisms.

3) They then <u>engulf</u> the microbes and <u>digest them</u>.

4) These white blood cells are <u>non-specific</u> — they attack <u>anything</u> that's not meant to be there.

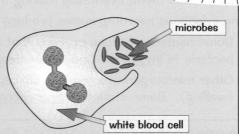

microbes

white blood cell

Antibodies <u>Recognise Foreign Microorganisms</u>

A different group of white blood cells attack <u>specific</u> microorganisms.

1) These white blood cells have receptors that recognise particular <u>antigens</u>. Antigens are substances that trigger <u>immune responses</u> — they're usually <u>protein</u> molecules on the surface of a <u>microorganism</u> cell.

2) Certain kinds of white blood cell produce <u>antibodies</u>. Antibodies are proteins that are <u>specific</u> to a particular antigen — <u>different microorganisms</u> have <u>different antigens</u>, so a different antibody is needed to recognise each different microorganism.

3) Antibodies <u>latch onto</u> invading microorganisms and do one of three things:

- They <u>mark</u> the microorganism so other <u>white blood cells</u> can engulf and digest it.
- They bind to and <u>neutralise</u> viruses or toxins.
- Some can even attach to bacteria and <u>kill them directly</u>.

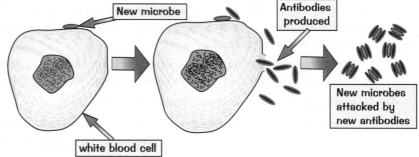

New microbe

Antibodies produced

New microbes attacked by new antibodies

white blood cell

4) Once the <u>right white blood cell</u> recognises the antigens on a microorganism, it <u>divides</u> to make <u>more identical cells</u>, which make lots of the right <u>antibody</u> to get on with fighting the infection.

5) Some white blood cells <u>stay around</u> in the blood after the original infection has been fought off — these are called <u>memory cells</u>.

6) Memory cells can <u>reproduce very quickly</u> if the <u>same</u> antigen enters the body for a <u>second</u> time.

7) The memory cells then produce loads of <u>antibodies</u> and kill off the microorganisms before you become ill — this is known as <u>immunity</u>.

<u>White blood cells are pretty handy...</u>

Have you ever noticed that loads of people seem to get <u>colds</u> as soon as they come back to school after the <u>summer holidays</u>? The reason is that people have been away on <u>holiday</u> and brought back new microorganisms that most people don't have the <u>antibodies</u> for.

Vaccination

Some diseases can be pretty nasty, so if possible you want to give your immune system a head start in fighting the microorganisms that cause it. You can do this using a vaccine.

Vaccinations Use a Safe Version of a Dangerous Microorganism

1) When you're infected with a new microorganism, it takes your white blood cells a few days to get their numbers up and to make the right antibodies to help them deal with it. By that time, you can get pretty ill.

2) Immunisation involves injecting dead or inactive microorganisms. These still carry the same antigens, which means your body produces antibodies to attack them — even though the microorganism is harmless (since it's dead or inactive).

3) The body also produces memory cells (see previous page) that recognise the antigens of the microorganisms and stay in the blood.

4) If live microorganisms of the same type appear after that, the memory cells can rapidly mass-produce antibodies to kill them off.

5) This normally means you can get rid of the disease-causing microorganisms before they reach a level that makes you sick.

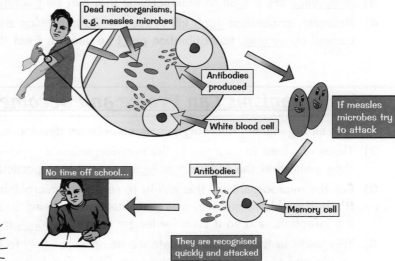

The MMR vaccine contains weakened versions of the viruses that cause measles, mumps and rubella (German measles) all together.

Epidemics can be Prevented by Vaccinating Lots of People

1) To prevent big outbreaks of diseases (called epidemics) a large percentage of the population needs to be vaccinated.

2) If a significant number of people aren't vaccinated, diseases can spread quickly through them and lots of people will be ill at the same time.

3) But if most people are vaccinated, even the people who aren't vaccinated are unlikely to catch the disease because there are fewer people able to pass it on.

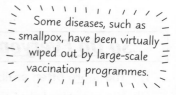
Some diseases, such as smallpox, have been virtually wiped out by large-scale vaccination programmes.

Vaccines and Drugs have Different Effects on Different People

1) Vaccines and drugs can never be completely safe for everyone. People can have side effects when using them, but these can be more serious for some people than others. For example, 1 in 4 children who have the meningitis vaccination develop a painful swelling at the site of the injection, and 1 in 50 have a fever after the vaccine.

2) Genetic differences also mean that people react differently to drugs and vaccines. For example, anaesthetics are drugs that stop people from feeling pain, e.g. during operations. Genetic differences mean that the length of time people are affected by anaesthetics is different.

An injection of dead microorganisms — roll on my next vaccine...

Prevention is better than cure, as they say — which is why vaccines are fantastic and much better than twiddling your thumbs, waiting to get those memory cells naturally. It's a bit of a shame that not everybody loves being viciously assaulted by a nurse with a needle — I do, personally, but that is a story for another time...

Antimicrobials

The discovery of antimicrobials, like penicillin, has been a huge benefit to medicine — suddenly infections that had often been fatal could be cured. But unfortunately they might not be a permanent solution.

Antimicrobials Can Inhibit or Kill Bacteria, Fungi and Viruses

1) Antimicrobials are chemicals that inhibit the growth of microorganisms or kill them, without seriously damaging your own body cells.

2) They're very useful for clearing up infections that your own immune system is having trouble with.

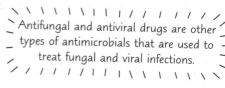
Antifungal and antiviral drugs are other types of antimicrobials that are used to treat fungal and viral infections.

3) Antibiotics are a type of antimicrobial that can kill bacteria.

4) However, antibiotics don't kill viruses — flu and colds are caused by viruses, so antibiotics can't be used to treat them.

Microorganisms Can Evolve and Become Resistant to Antimicrobials...

1) Like all organisms, microorganisms sometimes develop random mutations in their DNA.

2) These can lead to changes in the microorganism's characteristics. Sometimes, they mean that the organism is less affected by a particular antimicrobial.

3) For the microorganism, this ability to resist antimicrobials is a big advantage. It's better able to survive, even in a host who's being treated to get rid of the infection, and so it lives for longer and reproduces many more times.

4) This leads to the gene for resistance being passed on to lots of offspring — it's just natural selection (see page 30). This is how it spreads and becomes more common in a population of microorganisms over a period of time.

5) This is a problem for people who become infected with these microorganisms, because you can't easily get rid of them with antimicrobials. Sometimes drug companies can come up with new antimicrobials that are effective, but 'superbugs' that are resistant to most known antimicrobials are becoming more common (e.g. MRSA).

...So Do Everyone a Favour and Always Finish Your Antibiotics

1) The more often antibiotics are used, the bigger the problem of antibiotic-resistance becomes.

2) It's important that people only use antibiotics when they really need to:

> It's not that antibiotics actually cause resistance, but they do create a situation where naturally resistant bacteria have an advantage and so increase in numbers. If they're not doing you any good, it's pointless to take antibiotics — and it could be harmful for everyone else.

3) It's also important that you take all the antibiotics a doctor prescribes for you:

> Lots of people stop bothering to take their antibiotics as soon as they feel better, but this can increase the risk of antibiotic resistant bacteria emerging.

Aaargh, a giant earwig! Run from the attack of the superbug...

The reality of superbugs is possibly even scarier than giant earwigs. Actually, nothing's more scary than giant earwigs, but microorganisms that are resistant to all our drugs are a worrying thought. It'll be like going back in time to before antimicrobials were invented. So far new drugs have kept us one step ahead, but some people think it's only a matter of time until the options run out.

Drug Trials

Any new drug has to be <u>tested</u> to make sure it's <u>safe</u> to use, and to make sure it <u>does</u> what it claims to do.

Drugs are Tested First in a Laboratory

1) <u>New drugs</u> are being developed all the time to help fight different diseases.

2) These drugs are often developed using <u>human cells</u> that are grown in the lab. This means that you can measure the effect the drug has on real <u>human</u> cells.

3) On the other hand, it <u>can't</u> recreate the conditions of a <u>whole system</u> or <u>organism</u>, so you still can't be sure that the drug's <u>safe</u> to use, or that it <u>actually works</u>.

4) To make sure, all new drugs must be tested on at least two different species of <u>live mammal</u> (rats and monkeys are often used) before it's given to humans. This way, potentially <u>harmful</u> substances are usually weeded out before the drugs are given to <u>human volunteers</u>.

5) Many mammals have <u>systems</u> that are <u>similar</u> to those of humans, so the tests give early indications of what the drug might do in the human body.

6) If the drug causes serious <u>problems</u> in the animals, the testing is <u>unlikely</u> to go any further, and this saves any humans from being harmed. Testing is also <u>stopped</u> if the drug is <u>not effective</u>.

Drugs are Then Tested on Humans in Clinical Trials

1) If the laboratory tests don't pick up on anything that could <u>limit</u> how useful the drug will be, it will then go on to be tested on <u>human volunteers</u>. These tests are called <u>clinical trials</u>.

2) First, the drug is tested for <u>safety</u> on <u>healthy</u> volunteers. This is to make sure it doesn't have any <u>harmful side effects</u> when the body is working normally. Sick people are likely to be more <u>vulnerable</u> to any damage the drug could do, which is why the drug isn't tested on them yet.

3) If the results of the tests on healthy volunteers are good, the drugs can be tested on people suffering from the <u>illness</u>. These are tests for both <u>safety</u> and <u>effectiveness</u>.

4) <u>Placebos</u> are usually used in human drug trials. These are 'fake' treatments which don't actually involve giving the drug to the patient. This is so you can <u>compare</u> a group of people who were given the <u>actual</u> drug with a group who were given the <u>placebo</u>. In some trials where patients are <u>seriously ill</u> placebos <u>aren't</u> used because it's <u>unethical</u> not to allow all patients to get the potential benefits of the new drug.

5) If the drug <u>works</u>, the results should show that the condition of the volunteers in the group given the real drug <u>improved more</u> than those in the group given the placebo. If there are <u>side effects</u> associated with taking the drug, e.g. drowsiness, then the patients in the group taking the real drug will report feeling these <u>more</u> than the patients taking the placebo.

6) There are three human trials you need to know about — '<u>blind</u>', '<u>double-blind</u>' and '<u>open-label</u>' trials:

In <u>blind trials</u>, patients <u>don't know</u> if they've been given the drug or a placebo. This is because a patient who knows they're being treated might feel better for <u>psychological reasons</u>, even if there <u>hasn't</u> really been an improvement. In the same way a patient who knows they're <u>not</u> being treated might <u>not</u> feel better even if they <u>are</u> recovering. Blind trials <u>eliminate</u> these effects.

In <u>double-blind trials</u>, even the <u>scientists</u> carrying out the research don't find out until the end which patients got real drugs and which got placebos. This is so the scientists <u>monitoring</u> the patients and <u>analysing</u> the results aren't <u>subconsciously influenced</u> by their knowledge.

In <u>open-label trials</u>, both the <u>patients</u> and the research <u>scientists</u> are <u>aware</u> of the treatments that have been used. Open-label trials are used when you can't <u>mask</u> the treatments being tested, e.g. if one is a drug and another is exercise.

7) <u>Human drug trials</u> usually last a very <u>long time</u>, but it's important that they do. In some cases it takes a <u>while</u> for a drug to have the <u>effect</u> it was designed for, e.g. treating cancer. It's also important to find out if a drug has any <u>side effects</u> which may only appear after a <u>long time</u>.

Blind trials used to test new eye drops...

A trial in London in March 2006 left six men <u>seriously ill</u> after a new anti-inflammatory drug caused 'completely unanticipated' effects. But then, if nobody ever took part in trials, there would <u>never</u> be any <u>new drugs</u>.

The Circulatory System

Blood is vital. It moves oxygen from your lungs to your cells, carbon dioxide from your cells to your lungs, nutrients from your gut to your cells, hormones from your glands to your cells... oh, I'm exhausted.

The Heart and Blood Vessels Supply Blood to the Body

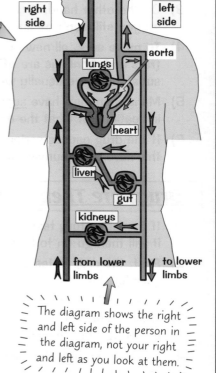

1) Blood is circulated around the body in tubes called blood vessels. Oxygen and nutrients are carried in the blood to the body cells, and waste substances such as carbon dioxide are carried away from the cells.

2) The heart is a pumping organ that keeps the blood flowing through the vessels. It's actually a double pump — the right side pumps deoxygenated blood to the lungs to collect oxygen and remove carbon dioxide. The left side pumps the oxygenated blood around the body.

3) The heart's made up of muscle cells that keep it beating continually. These cells need their own blood supply to deliver the nutrients and oxygen needed to keep the heart beating continually.

4) Blood is supplied to the heart by two coronary arteries, which branch from the base of the aorta (the biggest artery in the body).

The diagram shows the right and left side of the person in the diagram, not your right and left as you look at them.

There are Three Major Types of Blood Vessel

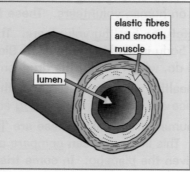

1) Arteries carry blood away from the heart to the body cells (including the heart muscle).

2) It comes out of the heart at high pressure, so the artery walls have to be strong and elastic. They're much thicker than the walls of veins...

elastic fibres and smooth muscle

lumen

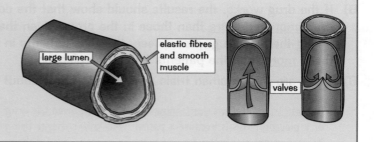

1) Veins carry blood back to the heart.

2) The blood is at a lower pressure in the veins so the walls don't need to be as thick.

3) They have a bigger lumen than arteries, to help the blood flow more easily.

4) They also have valves to help keep the blood flowing in the right direction.

large lumen

elastic fibres and smooth muscle

valves

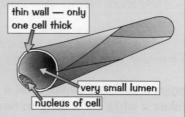

1) Capillaries are branches of arteries that are really tiny — you need a microscope to see them.

2) They carry the blood really close to every cell in the body to exchange substances with them.

3) They have permeable walls, so substances can diffuse in and out.

4) They supply nutrients and oxygen, and take away wastes like CO_2.

5) Their walls are only one cell thick. This increases the rate of diffusion by decreasing the distance over which it happens.

thin wall — only one cell thick

very small lumen

nucleus of cell

Unbreak my heart — say it's pumping again...

Don't forget that the heart is a double pump that has two jobs — pumping blood to the body, and to the lungs. From two jobs, to three blood vessels — you need to know how their structures help them with their functions.

Heart Rate and Blood Pressure

Your blood has got to travel a <u>long way</u> around your body and the only way it can do this is if it's <u>under pressure</u>. Your heart <u>beats</u> continuously to keep the blood moving and keep up this pressure.

Your Pulse Rate Can be Used to Measure Your Heart Rate

1) Your <u>heart rate</u> is the number of times your <u>heart beats</u> in <u>one minute</u> — it's measured in <u>BPM</u> (beats per minute).

2) Your <u>pulse rate</u> is the number of times an <u>artery pulsates</u> in <u>one minute</u>.

3) The pulsation of an artery is <u>caused</u> by blood being <u>pumped</u> through it by a <u>heart beat</u>, so you can measure your pulse rate to work out your <u>heart rate</u>.

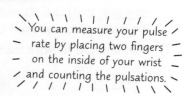
You can measure your pulse rate by placing two fingers on the inside of your wrist and counting the pulsations.

Blood is Pumped Around Your Body Under Pressure

Well, your blood pressure is a little high...

1) When your heart muscle <u>contracts</u>, blood is forced out of the heart — this <u>increases</u> the <u>pressure</u> of your blood. When your heart muscle <u>relaxes</u>, the heart fills with blood and your <u>blood pressure decreases</u>.

2) You can <u>measure</u> your blood pressure by taking a reading of the <u>pressure</u> of the blood <u>against the walls</u> of an <u>artery</u>.

3) Blood pressure measurements have <u>two values</u>, e.g. a person's blood pressure might be written as "135 over 85". The <u>higher</u> value is the pressure of the blood when the heart <u>contracts</u>, and the <u>lower</u> value is the pressure of the blood when the heart <u>relaxes</u>.

> A person's <u>heart rate</u> and <u>blood pressure</u> can be used to check how <u>healthy</u> they are by <u>comparing</u> their measurements against <u>"normal" measurements</u>.
>
> Normal measurements are usually given as a <u>range</u> of values because <u>individuals vary</u>, e.g. a normal resting heart rate for an adult is between 60 and 100 beats a minute.

High Blood Pressure Increases the Risk of Heart Disease

1) The <u>inner lining</u> of an artery is usually <u>smooth</u> and <u>unbroken</u>, but <u>high blood pressure</u> can <u>damage</u> it.

2) <u>Fatty deposits</u> can sometimes <u>build up</u> in damaged areas of arteries — these deposits <u>restrict</u> blood flow and cause the <u>blood pressure</u> in arteries to <u>increase</u>.

3) If a fatty deposit <u>breaks through</u> the inner lining of an artery, a <u>blood clot</u> may form around it.

4) The <u>blood clot</u> could <u>block</u> the artery completely, or it could <u>break away</u> and block a <u>different artery</u>.

5) If a <u>coronary artery</u> (see previous page) becomes <u>completely blocked</u> an area of the heart muscle will be totally <u>cut off</u> from its blood supply, receiving <u>no oxygen</u>. This causes a <u>heart attack</u>.

6) A heart attack can cause <u>serious damage</u> to the heart or may even cause the <u>death</u> of the <u>heart muscle</u> — which can be <u>fatal</u>.

Heart disease is just any disease that affects the heart — including heart attacks.

Don't let exam stress send your blood pressure through the roof...

This page started off nice enough — measuring your <u>pulse rate</u> is something you can do at home, and having your <u>blood pressure</u> taken is always fun. But then it got serious... and it doesn't get much more serious than <u>heart disease</u>. At least now you should understand why having <u>high blood pressure</u> is <u>not</u> a good thing.

Heart Disease

Some diseases are caused by <u>microorganisms</u>, but that's <u>not</u> usually the case with <u>heart disease</u>...

Lifestyle Factors <u>Can Increase the Risk</u> of Heart Disease

1) Heart disease can often be linked to <u>lifestyle factors</u>, such as what someone <u>eats</u> and how much <u>exercise</u> they do. Some people might be more at risk because of their <u>genes</u> too. In most people it's a condition caused by one or both of these things.

2) The lifestyle factors that <u>increase</u> the risk of heart disease include:

Poor diet

1) <u>Cholesterol</u> makes up a large part of the <u>fatty deposits</u> that can form in damaged arteries (see previous page).

2) This means that if the blood cholesterol level is <u>high</u> then the risk of heart disease is <u>increased</u>.

3) <u>High blood cholesterol</u> level is linked to eating foods high in <u>saturated fat</u>, e.g. fatty meats and cheese.

4) A diet <u>high in salt</u> also <u>increases</u> the risk of heart disease because it increases <u>blood pressure</u>.

Stress

1) People feel stress when they are <u>under pressure</u>, e.g. if they have a lot of work to do in a short amount of time.

2) If a person is stressed for a long period of time it can <u>increase</u> their <u>blood pressure</u> and so <u>increase</u> the risk of heart disease.

Smoking

1) Both <u>carbon monoxide</u> and <u>nicotine</u>, found in cigarette smoke, <u>increase</u> the risk of heart disease.

2) Carbon monoxide <u>reduces</u> the amount of <u>oxygen</u> the blood can transport. If <u>heart muscle</u> doesn't receive enough oxygen it can lead to a <u>heart attack</u> (see previous page).

3) Nicotine increases <u>heart rate</u>. The heart contracts more often increasing <u>blood pressure</u>, which increases the risk of <u>heart disease</u>.

Misuse of illegal drugs

Drugs like <u>ecstasy</u> and <u>cannabis</u> can also <u>increase</u> the risk of heart disease by causing an <u>increase</u> in <u>heart rate</u>, which increases <u>blood pressure</u>.

Excessive alcohol drinking

Drinking too much alcohol <u>increases</u> the risk of heart disease because it also <u>increases blood pressure</u>.

3) <u>Regular moderate exercise</u> reduces the risk of developing heart disease. This is because exercise <u>burns fat</u>, preventing it building up in the arteries. Exercise also <u>strengthens</u> the heart muscle.

4) Heart disease is more common in <u>industrialised countries</u>, such as the UK and USA, than in non-industrialised countries. This is mainly because people in these countries can <u>afford</u> a lot of high-fat food and often <u>don't need</u> to be very physically active.

Epidemiological Studies <u>Can Identify Possible</u> Risk Factors

Epidemiology is the study of <u>patterns</u> of diseases and the <u>factors</u> that affect them. You need to know about how epidemiological studies are used to identify the factors that increase the risk of <u>heart disease</u>.

1) Epidemiological studies can help to identify the <u>lifestyle risk factors</u>. For example, you could study a group of people who all died from heart disease to look for <u>similarities</u> in their lifestyle that may be <u>linked</u> to heart disease, e.g. they were all smokers or they all had a poor diet.

2) They can also involve large scale <u>genetics studies</u> to identify the <u>genetic risk factors</u>. For example, you could map the genetic makeup of a large group of people, then see if there are any <u>genetic similarities</u> between the people who are affected by heart disease.

Contrary to popular belief, lard sandwiches won't keep your heart healthy...

Time for a little bit of <u>common sense</u> — if you know the things that <u>increase</u> the risk of heart disease, <u>cut down on them</u> by changing your lifestyle. It's <u>not</u> rocket science, but it's important that you're aware of it.

Homeostasis — The Basics

Homeostasis — a word that strikes fear into the heart of many a GCSE student. But it's really not that bad at all. This page is a brief introduction to the topic, so you need to nail all of this before you can move on.

Homeostasis — Maintaining a Constant Internal Environment

1) Homeostasis is all about balancing inputs (stuff going into your body) with outputs (stuff leaving) to maintain a constant internal environment.

2) The conditions inside your body need to be kept steady, even when the external environment changes. This is really important because your cells need the right conditions in order to function properly.

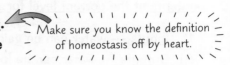

Make sure you know the definition of homeostasis off by heart.

3) You have loads of automatic control systems in your body that regulate your internal environment — these include both nervous and hormonal communication systems. For example, there's a control system that maintains your water content (see pages 26-27) and one that maintains your body temperature.

I'm not really a doctor — this clipboard isn't holding anything. But take it from me, homeostasis is one important topic.

4) All your automatic control systems are made up of three main components which work together to maintain a steady condition — receptors, processing centres and effectors.

Negative Feedback Counteracts Changes

Your automatic control systems keep your internal environment stable using a mechanism called negative feedback. When the level of something (e.g. water or temperature) gets too high or too low, your body uses negative feedback to bring it back to normal.

1) Receptor detects a change in the environment — level is too high.

2) The processing centre receives the information and coordinates a response.

3) Effector produces a response, which counteracts the change — the level decreases.

level decreases   level increases

1) Receptor detects a change in the environment — level is too low.

2) The processing centre receives the information and coordinates a response.

3) Effector produces a response, which counteracts the change — the level increases.

The effectors will just carry on producing the responses for as long as they're stimulated by the processing centre. This might cause the opposite problem — making the level change too much (away from the ideal). Luckily the receptor detects if the level becomes too different and negative feedback starts again.

This process happens without you thinking about it — it's all automatic.

Homeostasis — I always thought that was Latin for static caravan...

See, it wasn't so bad, was it? OK, the bit about negative feedback might have confused you at first, but the more you go over it, the more it makes sense. Make sure you've got your head around this page because the next two pages are all about how your body controls the amount of water inside it. It'll be fun — weeeeee...

Controlling Water Content

The <u>kidneys</u> are really important in this whole homeostasis thing — they help regulate <u>water content</u>.

Balancing Water Level is Really Important

The <u>water level</u> in your cells is very <u>important</u> — your body needs to maintain the <u>concentration</u> of its <u>cell contents</u> at the <u>correct level</u> for <u>cell activity</u>. So your body needs to <u>balance</u> the <u>inputs</u> and the <u>outputs</u>...

1) <u>Inputs</u> — water can be gained from drinks, food and respiration.
2) <u>Outputs</u> — water can be lost through sweating, breathing, in faeces and in urine.

Kidneys Help Balance Substances in the Body

The kidneys are pretty useful organs as they play a vital role in <u>balancing levels</u> of <u>water</u>, <u>waste</u> and <u>other chemicals</u> in the body. To balance these levels the kidneys do the following things...

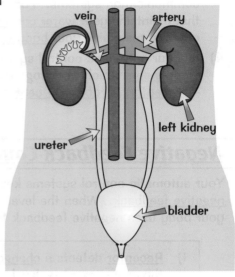

1) They <u>filter small molecules</u> from the <u>blood</u>, including <u>water</u>, <u>sugar</u>, <u>salt</u> and <u>waste</u>.

2) They <u>reabsorb</u> various things...

- All the <u>sugar</u>.
- As much <u>salt</u> and <u>water</u> as the body requires. Water absorption is controlled by the level of the hormone <u>ADH</u> (see next page)

3) Whatever isn't reabsorbed forms <u>urine</u>, which is excreted by the kidneys and stored in the <u>bladder</u>.

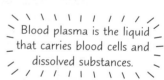

Blood plasma is the liquid that carries blood cells and dissolved substances.

Your Urine isn't Always the Same

The kidneys balance water levels by producing <u>dilute</u> or <u>concentrated urine</u>. The concentration of the urine depends on the <u>concentration of the blood plasma</u>, which can vary with the external temperature, exercise level, and the intake of fluids and salt.

1) External temperature

Temperature affects the amount you sweat. Sweat contains water so sweating causes <u>water loss</u>. This means when it's hot the kidneys will <u>reabsorb</u> more water back into the blood. This leaves only a small amount of water — so only a <u>small amount</u> of quite <u>concentrated</u> urine will be produced.

2) Exercise

Exercise makes you <u>hotter</u>, so you <u>sweat</u> to cool down. This produces the same effect as heat — a <u>concentrated</u>, <u>small volume</u> of urine.

3) Intake of fluids and salts

Not drinking enough water or eating too much salt will produce <u>concentrated</u> urine (since there'll be little excess water to 'dilute' the other wastes). Drinking lots of water will produce <u>lots</u> of <u>dilute</u> urine.

Reabsorb those facts and excrete the excess...

On average, the kidneys filter <u>1500 litres</u> of blood a day (you only have 4-6 litres of blood in your body — it just goes through the kidneys about <u>300 times</u>). And the kidneys excrete <u>1.5 litres</u> of urine a day. So that's <u>547.5 litres</u> of wee a <u>year</u>... that's <u>five baths</u> full... not that I'm suggesting you put it there.

Controlling Water Content

Controlling water content is pretty important — so here's another page about <u>urine</u>. Just for you.

The <u>Concentration of Urine</u> <u>is Controlled</u> <u>by a</u> <u>Hormone</u>

1) The concentration of urine is controlled by a hormone called <u>anti-diuretic hormone</u> (ADH). This is released into the <u>bloodstream</u> by the <u>pituitary gland</u>.

2) The brain <u>monitors the water content of the blood</u> and instructs the <u>pituitary gland</u> to release <u>ADH</u> into the blood according to how much is needed.

3) The whole process of water content regulation is controlled by <u>negative feedback</u> (see page 25). This means that if the water content gets <u>too high</u> or <u>too low</u> a mechanism will be triggered that brings it back to <u>normal</u>.

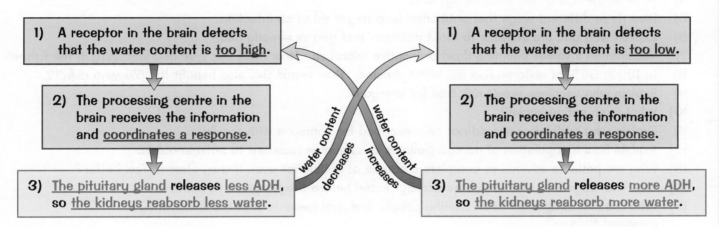

So, using negative feedback the amount of water in your body can be closely regulated. Don't forget that the <u>more water</u> your kidneys reabsorb, the <u>less water</u> will pass out as <u>urine</u>.

ADH Production <u>can be Affected by</u> <u>Drugs</u>

ADH production is usually regulated by the negative feedback mechanism. However, some drugs can <u>interfere</u> with the natural state of affairs — affecting your <u>urine</u>. Nice.

Alcohol Suppresses **ADH Production**

1) Drinking <u>alcohol</u> can result in a <u>larger amount</u> of <u>more dilute</u> urine (than normal) being produced.

2) Alcohol suppresses the <u>production of ADH</u>, so the kidneys will <u>reabsorb less</u> water.

3) This means <u>more water</u> passes out of the body as <u>urine</u>, which can cause <u>dehydration</u>. This can be <u>harmful</u> to your health, e.g. dehydration can cause headaches and dizziness and can eventually lead to death.

Ecstasy Increases **ADH Production**

1) <u>Ecstasy</u> is an illegal recreational drug. Taking ecstasy can result in a <u>smaller amount</u> of <u>more concentrated</u> urine (than normal) being produced.

2) Ecstasy causes the <u>production of ADH</u> to <u>increase</u>, so the kidneys will <u>reabsorb more</u> water.

3) This means that <u>less water</u> can pass out of the body as <u>urine</u>.

<u>Bet you didn't realise wee is so exciting...</u>

Scientists have made a machine that can do the kidney's job for us — a <u>kidney dialysis machine</u>. People with <u>kidney failure</u> have to use it for 3-4 hours, 3 times a week. Unfortunately it's not something you can carry around in your back pocket, which makes life <u>difficult</u> for people with kidney failure.

Revision Summary for Module B2

Congratulations, that's another chunk of biology under your belt. But before you do the most satisfying stretch in the world, I've got a little gift for you... a whole bunch of questions to test just how much of this section you've got to grips with. Don't be sad if you get any wrong — just go back and have another read of the topic and be glad that you're finding out what you do and don't know before the exam. Once you've got them all right, feel free to bend your limbs into weird shapes and let out yelps of joy.

1) Describe two ways that microorganisms can cause the symptoms of an infectious disease.
2) Explain why bacteria can reproduce rapidly inside the human body.
3)* If you start with one bacterium that reproduces every 40 minutes, how many bacteria will you have after 6 hours?
4) What is the role of the immune system?
5) Give three different ways that antibodies help to get rid of an infection.
6) Explain why you are immune to most diseases that you've already had.
7) Vaccination involves injecting dead or inactive microbes. How does this give you immunity in the future?
8) In 1993, 95% of children had the MMR vaccine. How would this also benefit the 5% who didn't?
9) Explain why vaccines aren't risk free for everyone.
10) What is an antimicrobial?
11) Explain why antibiotics should not be prescribed for someone with the flu.
12) Explain how a population of microorganisms can become resistant to antimicrobials.
13) Why are patients advised to complete a course of antibiotics even if they start to feel better?
14) Give two ways that new drugs are usually tested before they're given to humans.
15) Why are new drugs tested on healthy people first, not patients with the illness they're designed to cure?
16) Explain what a placebo is.
17) What is a double-blind clinical trial?
18) Explain the importance of long-term human drug trials.
19) The heart is a double pump. Explain what this means.
20) How is the structure of an artery adapted to its function?
21) How is the structure of a vein adapted to its function?
22) How is the structure of a capillary adapted to its function?
23) Explain why a person's heart rate can be measured by taking their pulse rate.
24) When a blood pressure measurement is taken, what is actually being measured?
25) Describe one way that high blood pressure can cause heart disease.
26)*Have a look at the table below:

Name	Occupation	Cigarettes per day	Exercise per week	Favourite meal
Tricia	Florist	0	5 hours	Houmous and pitta bread
Dave	Stock broker	40	20 minutes	Cheeseburger and chips

    a) Who is more at risk from heart disease, Tricia or Dave? Give two reasons for your answer.

    b) Give two ways of reducing the risk of heart disease.

27) Explain how epidemiological studies can be used to identify the risk factors for heart disease.
28) What is homeostasis?
29) Name the three main components of the body's automatic control systems.
30) Give two ways that water is gained by the body.
31) What factors can affect the concentration of urine produced by the kidneys?
32) Which gland releases ADH?
33) If there is an increase in water content in the blood, will more or less ADH be released?
34) What effect does alcohol have on urine production?

* Answers on page 84.

Adaptation and Variation

Life on Earth — I can't imagine what we'd do without it... well, we wouldn't exist at all I suppose.

Learn This Definition of a Species First...

Trust me, getting your head round this definition will help you to understand all the other stuff in the section:

A SPECIES is a group of organisms that can breed together to produce fertile offspring.

Species Adapt to Their Environments

Animal and plant species survive in many different environments — they can do this because they have adapted to their environment. Adaptations make individuals of a species more likely to survive and go on to produce offspring — this makes it more likely that the whole species will continue to exist in its environment. Here are a couple of examples of how organisms have adapted to their environment:

You might have to work out how different organisms are adapted to their environment in your exam.

The Cactus is Well Adapted for Hot, Dry (Desert) Conditions

1) Cacti have a rounded shape, giving them a small surface area compared to their volume to reduce water loss.

2) They've got a thick waxy layer (called a cuticle) and leaves reduced to spines to further reduce water loss.

3) They store water in their thick stem, which they can use to survive when there's not much around.

4) They have shallow but very extensive roots. This ensures water is absorbed quickly over a large area.

Fish are Adapted to Aquatic Environments

1) Fish have gills that extract oxygen from water for respiration.

2) They have tail fins with a large surface area to propel them through the water. They use their other fins to keep them stable as they move.

3) The bodies of fish are streamlined so they can move through water with as little resistance as possible.

4) Fish have an organ called a swim bladder (or air bladder). They can adjust the amount of gas in their swim bladder to change their depth in the water without having to use any energy.

Individuals of the Same Species Have Differences

1) Individuals of the same species will usually look at least slightly different — e.g. in a room full of people you'll see different colour hair, individually shaped noses, a variety of heights etc.

2) These differences are called the variation within a species. Some of this variation is genetic so it can be passed on to the individual's offspring.

3) One of the causes of genetic variation is when genes change.

4) These changes are called mutations — they happen all the time. Mutations can be caused by outside factors like radiation or chemicals, and by mistakes when genes are copied during cell division.

5) If mutations occur in body cells, they usually have little or no effect, though they can lead to cancer.

6) If they occur during the formation of sex cells, they have more effect because the mutation will then be passed on to all the cells of the offspring.

7) This can cause offspring to develop new characteristics. Some of these characteristics might be harmful to the organism, but others might actually help them to survive.

Variety is the spice of life — or is it paprika...

It's important to remember that genetic variation that arises from mutations can be passed on to offspring.

Natural Selection

Natural selection's about how variation causes a species to change over time.
This helps the organisms to become better adapted to their environment.

Natural Selection Means the "Survival of the Fittest"

Natural selection is the process that causes evolution. It works like this:

1) Living things show genetic variation — they're not all the same. OK, it's fairly simple so far.

2) The resources living things need to survive are limited. Individuals must compete for these resources to survive — only some of the individuals will survive.

3) Some of the varieties of a particular species will have a better chance of survival. Those varieties will then have an increased chance of reproducing and passing on their genes.

4) This means that a greater proportion of individuals in the next generation will have the characteristics that help the organisms to survive.

5) Over many generations, the species becomes better and better able to survive. The 'best' features are naturally selected and the species becomes more and more adapted to its environment.

HERE'S AN EXAMPLE

Once upon a time maybe all rabbits had short ears and managed OK. Then one day out popped a rabbit with big ears who could hear better and was always the first to dive for cover at the sound of a predator. Pretty soon he's fathered a whole family of rabbits with big ears, all diving for cover before the other rabbits, and before you know it there are only big-eared rabbits left — because the rest just didn't hear trouble coming quick enough.

This is how populations adapt to survive better in their environment (an organism doesn't actually change when it's alive — changes only occur from generation to generation).

Over many generations the characteristic that increases survival becomes more common in the population.

FOX!

Selective Breeding is Where Humans Choose What Gets Selected

Selective breeding involves humans deliberately choosing a feature they want to appear in the next generation and only breeding from animals or plants that have it. Unlike natural selection, which only selects features that help survival, selective breeding may promote features that don't help survival.

For example, a breeder might choose to only breed from the cows that produce the most milk, so that future generations of cows produce more milk than previous generations. This doesn't help the cow survive — instead it helps the farmer to make money.

Sniff sniff... you only want me for my milk.

"Natural Selection" — sounds like vegan chocolates...

If you like this page, you're (probably) going to love the next one — but make sure you've got all the natural selection stuff clear in your head before you move on. Trust us humans to find a way to tamper with natural selection — hmm, I wonder how long it would take for humans to evolve eyes in the backs of our heads...

Evolution

There are <u>lots of species</u> around these days, and the <u>evidence</u> shows that evolution's how they all came about.

Somehow, a Long Time Ago, Life Must Have Started

1) Scientists estimate that <u>life</u> on Earth <u>began</u> about <u>3500 million years ago</u>.
2) Today, there's an <u>enormous</u> number of <u>species</u> on Earth.
3) There are also loads of species that have become <u>extinct</u> so, since life began, a huge number of different living things have existed on the planet.
4) The very <u>first</u> living things were very <u>simple</u>. Life then evolved to become more <u>complex</u> and <u>varied</u>.
5) All living things that exist now, and have ever existed, <u>evolved</u> from those very simple <u>early life forms</u>.

There are different ideas about how life first appeared.

The Process of Evolution can Produce New Species

Sometimes, groups of organisms of the same species become <u>isolated</u> from each other so they can't <u>interbreed</u>, e.g. two populations of the same species might be on two different islands. A number of factors can then <u>combine</u> to make the two groups of organisms so different that they become two <u>different species</u>.

1) Different <u>mutations</u> create different <u>new features</u> in the two groups of organisms.
2) <u>Natural selection</u> works on the new features so that, if they are of <u>benefit</u>, they <u>spread</u> through each of the populations.
3) <u>Environmental changes</u> also play a part. For example, if the climate changes in one area, but not another, then organisms of the same species in the two areas will develop <u>different adaptations</u> to the different conditions that they live in.

There is Good Evidence for Evolution

If you're going to say that living things <u>evolved</u> from very simple life forms, you need to find good <u>evidence</u> for it. <u>Fossil records</u> and <u>DNA</u> both provide <u>evidence</u> for evolution:

1) There is evidence for evolution in the <u>fossil record</u>, which shows species getting more and more <u>complex</u> as time goes on.
2) <u>DNA</u> controls the <u>characteristics</u> of living things. It also <u>mutates</u> and changes over time. All living things have some <u>similarities</u> in their DNA, as you would expect if they have all <u>evolved</u> from the <u>same</u> simple life forms. The more <u>closely related</u> two species are, the more <u>similar</u> their DNA is. Scientists can use the <u>similarities and differences</u> in DNA to work out how life has <u>evolved</u>.

Evolution by Natural Selection Was a Revolutionary Idea

1) <u>Charles Darwin</u> proposed the theory of evolution by <u>natural selection</u>, which he came up with by making <u>many observations</u> of organisms and applying <u>creative thought</u> to his findings.
2) But Darwin wasn't the only person to think about how evolution happens — a French chap called <u>Lamarck</u> had a different idea:

<u>Lamarck</u> argued that if a <u>characteristic</u> was <u>used a lot</u> by an animal then it would become more <u>developed</u>. Lamarck reckoned that these <u>acquired characteristics</u> could be passed on to the <u>animal's offspring</u>. For example, if a rabbit did a lot of running and developed big leg muscles, Lamarck believed that the rabbit's offspring would also have big leg muscles.

3) But people eventually concluded that acquired characteristics <u>don't</u> have a <u>genetic basis</u> — so they're <u>unable</u> to be passed on to the next generation. This is why Lamarck's theory was <u>rejected</u> in favour of Darwin's.

My brother has genetic similarities with worms and aliens...

The <u>development</u> of a new species takes a <u>long time</u> — it doesn't happen every day.

Biodiversity and Classification

Biodiversity's about the variety of life on Earth. There's so much variety in fact, that scientists have had to come up with a handy system of classification to help make sense of it all.

Earth's Biodiversity is Important

1) Biodiversity includes:
   - The number of different species on Earth.
   - The range of different types of organisms, e.g. microorganisms, plants and animals.
   - The genetic variation between organisms of the same species (for more on variation see page 29).

2) Maintaining biodiversity (by stopping species from becoming extinct) is important. Here's why:

   - The more plants we have available, the more resources there are for developing new food crops.
   - Many new medicines have been discovered using chemicals produced by living things. For example, digitalis, a drug used to treat heart disease, was discovered in the foxglove. When a living organism becomes extinct, the unique chemicals it produces are no longer available.

The Rate of Extinction of Species is Increasing

1) Many organisms have become extinct in the past, and many are threatened with extinction now.

2) The rate at which species are becoming extinct is increasing.

3) There is a correlation between the growth of the world's population and the number of species extinctions. This suggests that a lot of extinction is due to human activities.

4) In some cases, humans have caused extinction directly, e.g. the Tasmanian wolf was hunted to extinction.

5) Humans can also cause extinction indirectly by destroying an organism's habitat or by introducing new species which it cannot compete with.

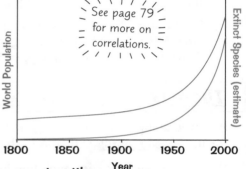

See page 79 for more on correlations.

Classification is all About Organising Organisms into Groups

Scientists group organisms together according to similarities in their characteristics — their genetics (i.e. the similarities in their DNA) and the physical features they have (e.g. all vertebrates have a skeleton with a backbone and plants can be classified by whether they have a flower or not).

1) All of the millions of species on Earth can be grouped into five different kingdoms — bacteria, fungi, algae, plants and animals.

2) Each kingdom is then divided into more groups, and they are divided into more groups until you get down to a species.

3) As you go down these groups, the number of types of organisms in each one decreases, but the number of characteristics that the organisms have in common increases.

Classification is Pretty Useful

1) Classification shows us the evolutionary relationships between different organisms. For example, two organisms that are in similar classification groups will share lots of genetic and structural characteristics, so it's likely that they both evolved from the same ancestor organism.

2) Evolutionary relationships can be shown for all living and fossilised organisms that have been classified.

Biodiversity — I think they were the ones who won that talent show...

Biodiversity's a useful thing, but the increasing rate of species extinction means that it's being reduced every day. But hey, at least when we can't develop any new crops or medicines we'll still have our nice classification system.

Interactions Between Organisms

Organisms are <u>dependent</u> on a number of other organisms and their environment for <u>survival</u>.

Every *Living Thing* Needs Resources *from its Environment*

The <u>environment</u> in which an organism lives provides it with <u>factors</u> that are <u>essential</u> for life. These include:

If any essential factor in a habitat is in <u>short supply</u>, the different species that need it have to <u>compete</u> for it. If there's not enough to go around, some organisms <u>won't survive</u>. This will <u>limit</u> the size of their populations in that habitat.

1) <u>Light</u> (needed by plants to make food)
2) <u>Food</u> (for animals) and <u>minerals</u> (for plants)
3) <u>Oxygen</u> (for animals and plants) and <u>carbon dioxide</u> (for plants)
4) <u>Water</u> (vital for all living organisms)

Organisms also depend on <u>other organisms</u> (usually for food) — this is called <u>interdependence</u>.

Any *Change* in *Any Environment* can Have *Knock-on Effects...*

The <u>interdependence</u> of all the living things in a habitat means that any major <u>change</u> in the habitat can have <u>far-reaching effects</u>.

The diagram on the right shows part of a <u>food web</u> (a diagram of what eats what) from a <u>stream</u>.

<u>Stonefly larvae</u> are particularly sensitive to <u>pollution</u>. Suppose pollution <u>killed</u> them in this stream. The table below shows some of the <u>effects</u> this might have on some of the other organisms in the food web.

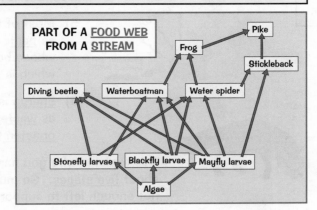

PART OF A <u>FOOD WEB</u> FROM A <u>STREAM</u>

Organism	Effect of loss of stonefly larvae	Effect on population
Blackfly larvae	Less competition for algae	Increase
	More likely to be eaten by predators	Decrease
Water spider	Less food	Decrease
Stickleback	Less food (if water spider or mayfly larvae numbers decrease)	Decrease

Remember that food webs are <u>very complex</u> and that these effects are difficult to predict accurately.

...Even Possibly Extinction

The fossil record contains many species that <u>don't exist any more</u>. For example, all the different species of <u>dinosaurs</u> and <u>mammoths</u> are extinct, with only <u>fossils</u> to tell us they existed at all.

<u>Rapid change</u> in the environment can cause a species to become <u>extinct</u>. Here are <u>three</u> changes that could cause extinction:

1) The <u>environmental conditions</u> change (e.g. destruction of habitat) and the species <u>can't adapt</u> to the change.

2) A new species is introduced which is a <u>competitor</u>, <u>disease organism</u> or <u>predator</u> of that species (this could include humans hunting them).

3) An organism in its <u>food web</u> that it is reliant on becomes <u>extinct</u>.

I'm dependent on the coffee plant...

If you're asked to analyse the <u>consequences</u> of a change in a food web, consider '<u>knock-on</u>' effects as well as the organisms which are directly affected. You'll find that there are loads of different possible things that could happen — so just be aware of all the <u>possibilities</u> and you'll be sure of good marks.

Energy in an Ecosystem

An <u>ecosystem</u> is all the <u>different organisms</u> living together in a <u>particular environment</u>. Sounds cosy.

Nearly <u>All</u> the <u>Energy</u> in an Ecosystem Comes From the <u>Sun</u>

1) Energy from the <u>Sun</u> is the source of energy for nearly <u>all</u> life on Earth.

2) <u>Plants</u> use a small percentage of the light energy from the Sun during photosynthesis. The light energy is <u>stored</u> by converting it to <u>chemicals</u> which make up <u>plants' cells</u>.

3) Energy is <u>transferred</u> between organisms in an ecosystem when animals eat plants and other animals. Energy is also transferred when <u>decay organisms</u> (decomposers and detritivores) feed on parts of <u>dead organisms</u> and <u>waste materials</u>.

4) Energy is <u>lost</u> at each stage — much of it is used for <u>staying alive</u>, i.e. in <u>respiration</u>, which powers all life processes.

5) Most of this energy is eventually <u>lost</u> to the surroundings as <u>heat</u>. This is especially true for <u>mammals</u> and <u>birds</u>, whose bodies must be kept at a <u>constant temperature</u> which is normally higher than their surroundings.

6) <u>Energy</u> is also lost at each stage of the food chain as <u>waste products</u> (e.g. droppings and urine) and <u>uneaten parts</u> of organisms (e.g. bones).

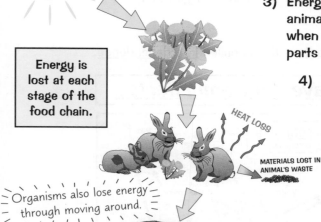

Energy is lost at each stage of the food chain.

HEAT LOSS

MATERIALS LOST IN ANIMAL'S WASTE

Organisms also lose energy through moving around.

This explains why you hardly ever get <u>food chains</u> with more than about <u>five stages</u>. So much <u>energy</u> is <u>lost</u> at each stage that there's not enough left to support more organisms after four or five stages.

You Need to be Able to <u>Interpret Data</u> on <u>Energy Flow</u>

rosebush: 80 000 kJ   greenfly: 10 000 kJ   ladybird: 900 kJ   bird: 40 kJ

1) The numbers show the <u>amount of energy</u> available to the <u>next stage</u> of a food chain. So <u>80 000 kJ</u> is the amount of energy available to the <u>greenfly</u>, and <u>10 000 kJ</u> is the amount available to the <u>ladybird</u>.

2) You can work out how much energy has been <u>lost</u> at each stage by taking away the energy that is available to the <u>next</u> stage from the energy that was available from the <u>previous</u> stage. Like this:
Energy <u>lost</u> at 1st stage = 80 000 kJ – 10 000 kJ = <u>70 000 kJ lost</u>.

3) You can also calculate the <u>efficiency of energy transfer</u> — this just means how good one stage is at passing on energy to the next stage.

$$\text{efficiency} = \frac{\text{energy available to the next stage}}{\text{energy that was available to the previous stage}} \times 100$$

So at the first stage,
<u>efficiency</u> of energy transfer
= 10 000 kJ ÷ 80 000 kJ × 100
= <u>12.5% efficient</u>.

Ecosystems are about as energy efficient as a 40W light bulb (the old kind)...

Energy is lost through <u>heat</u>, <u>waste products</u> and <u>uneaten parts</u> of organisms — food chains are <u>inefficient</u>.
Make sure you're efficient though, by learning how to calculate the <u>efficiency of energy transfer</u> in a food chain.

The Carbon Cycle

Carbon is constantly moving between the <u>atmosphere</u>, the <u>soil</u> and <u>living things</u> in the carbon cycle. Don't be put off by the diagram — this stuff is as easy as falling off a <u>bicycle</u>. OK, stop laughing and get learning...

The Carbon Cycle Shows How Carbon is Recycled

<u>Carbon</u> is an important element in the materials that living things are made from. It's constantly <u>recycled</u>:

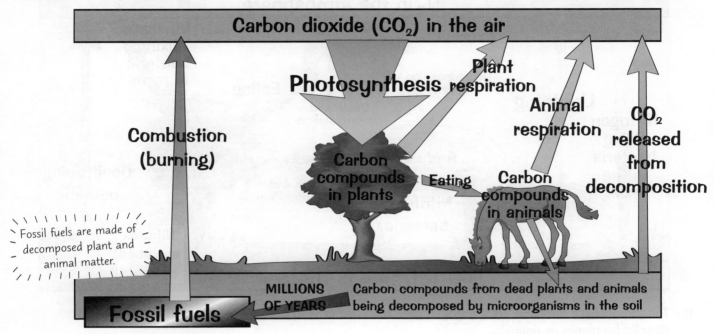

Carbon dioxide (CO_2) in the air

Photosynthesis Plant respiration

Animal respiration

CO_2 released from decomposition

Combustion (burning)

Carbon compounds in plants

Eating

Carbon compounds in animals

Fossil fuels are made of decomposed plant and animal matter.

Fossil fuels

MILLIONS OF YEARS

Carbon compounds from dead plants and animals being decomposed by microorganisms in the soil

You need to learn these important points:

1) There's only <u>one arrow</u> going <u>down</u>. The whole thing is powered by <u>photosynthesis</u>.

2) In photosynthesis <u>plants</u> convert the carbon from <u>CO_2</u> in the air into <u>sugars</u>.
    Plants can now incorporate this carbon into <u>carbohydrates</u>, <u>fats</u> and <u>proteins</u> as well.

3) <u>Eating</u> passes the carbon compounds in the plants along to <u>animals</u> in a food chain or web.

4) Both plant and animal <u>respiration</u> while the organisms are alive <u>releases CO_2</u> back into the <u>air</u>.

5) Plants and animals eventually <u>die</u> and <u>decompose</u>.

6) When plants and animals <u>decompose</u> they're broken down by <u>microorganisms</u>.
    These decomposers <u>release CO_2</u> back into the air by <u>respiration</u>
    as they break down the material.

7) The <u>combustion</u> (burning) of <u>fossil fuels</u> also releases CO_2 into the air.

Come on out, it's only a little carbon cycle, it can't hurt you...

Carbon is a very <u>important element</u> for living things — it's the basis for all the <u>organic molecules</u> (fats, proteins, carbohydrates etc.) in our bodies. In sci-fi programmes the aliens are sometimes silicon-based instead, but then they're usually defeated in the end by some generic action hero type anyway.

The Nitrogen Cycle

Nitrogen, just like carbon, is constantly being recycled. So the nitrogen in your proteins might once have been in the air. And before that it might have been in a plant. Or even in some horse wee. Nice.

Nitrogen is Recycled in the Nitrogen Cycle

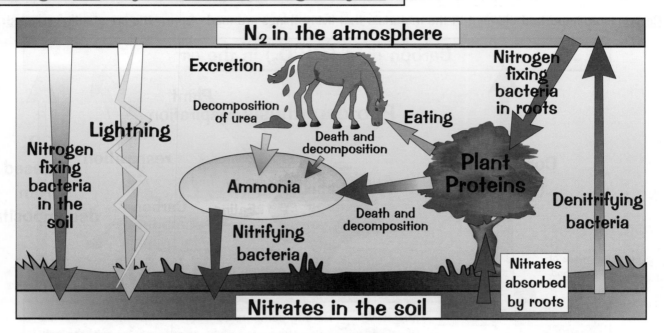

1) The atmosphere contains 78% nitrogen gas, N_2. This is very unreactive and so it can't be used directly by plants or animals.

2) Nitrogen is needed for making proteins for growth, so living organisms have to get it somehow.

3) Plants get their nitrogen from the soil but it needs to be turned into nitrates so they can use it to make proteins. Animals can only get proteins by eating plants (or each other).

4) Nitrogen fixation isn't an obsession with nitrogen — it's the process of turning N_2 from the air into nitrogen compounds (e.g. nitrates) in the soil which plants can use. There are two main ways that this happens:

   a) Lightning — there's so much energy in a bolt of lightning that it's enough to make nitrogen react with oxygen in the air to give nitrates.

   b) Nitrogen-fixing bacteria in roots and soil (see below).

5) Decomposers break down proteins in dead plants and animals, and urea in excreted animal waste, into ammonia. Ammonia is turned into nitrates by nitrifying bacteria that are found in soil.

6) There are four different types of microorganisms involved in the nitrogen cycle:

   a) DECOMPOSERS — decompose proteins and urea and turn them into ammonia.

   b) NITRIFYING BACTERIA — turn ammonia in decaying matter into nitrates (this is nitrification).

   c) NITROGEN-FIXING BACTERIA — turn atmospheric N_2 into nitrogen compounds that plants can use.

   d) DENITRIFYING BACTERIA — turn nitrates back into N_2 gas. This is of no benefit to living organisms.

It's the cyyyycle of liiiiife...

People sometimes forget that when we breathe in, we're breathing in mainly nitrogen. It's a pretty boring gas, colourless and with no taste or smell. But nitrogen is vital to living things, because the amino acids that join together to make proteins (like enzymes) all contain nitrogen.

Measuring Environmental Change

Environments are changing all the time and some of the changes can be measured. You need to know about how we use both non-living things and living things to measure environmental change...

Environmental Change can be Measured with Non-Living Indicators...

Here are three non-living indicators that you can use to measure environmental change:

Temperature

The temperature of an environment will vary all the time (e.g. throughout the day). However, temperature measurements taken using instruments (e.g. thermometers) over a long period of time could indicate that the climate of the environment is changing, e.g. global warming.

Nitrate level

Nitrate level can be used as an indicator of environmental change in a body of water. An increase in nitrate level could be caused by sewage or fertilisers entering the water — which could show that the water is being polluted.

You can monitor these non-living indictors using special probes and data-logging equipment.

Carbon dioxide (CO_2) level

CO_2 level can be used to measure environmental change in the air. An increase in CO_2 could be caused by lots of factors, including human activities such as burning fossil fuels. Increases in CO_2 increase the rate of global warming.

...and Living Indicators

Some organisms are very sensitive to changes in their environment — they can be used as living indicators of environmental change. For example:

Lichen

Air pollution can be monitored by looking at particular types of lichen, which are very sensitive to levels of sulfur dioxide in the atmosphere (and so can give a good idea about the level of pollution from car exhausts, power stations, etc.). The number and type of lichen at a particular location will indicate how clean the air is (e.g. the air is clean if there are lots of lichen).

Mayfly Nymphs

If raw sewage is released into a river, the bacterial population in the water increases and uses up the oxygen. Animals like mayfly nymphs are a good living indicator for water pollution, because they are very sensitive to the level of oxygen in the water. If you find mayfly nymphs in a river, it indicates that the water is clean.

Phytoplankton

Phytoplankton (microscopic algae that live in water) populations increase when the levels of nitrates and phosphates in the water increase — this is called an algal bloom. Adding fertilisers or sewage to rivers and lakes causes an increase in nitrates and phosphates, so algal blooms can be used to indicate water pollution.

Teenagers are a living indicator — not found in clean rooms...

In the exam, you might have to interpret data from living and non-living sources to investigate environmental change — so it'll be a good idea to learn this page, top to bottom.

Sustainability

Sustainability's a <u>tricky</u> one to get your head around, so make sure you have a <u>really good look</u> at this page.

Sustainability *Needs Careful* Planning

1) Human activities can <u>damage</u> the environment (e.g. pollution). And some of the damage we do can't easily be <u>repaired</u> (e.g. the destruction of the rainforests). This means the environment won't be the same for <u>future generations</u>.

2) We're also placing <u>greater pressure</u> on our planet's <u>limited resources</u>, e.g. we use fossil fuels, but they'll eventually <u>run out</u>. This means that the resources won't be around for future generations to <u>use</u>.

3) So we need to <u>plan carefully</u> to make sure that our activities today don't mess things up for future generations — this is the idea behind <u>sustainability</u>...

> <u>SUSTAINABILITY</u> means meeting the needs of <u>today's</u> population <u>without</u> harming the environment so that <u>future</u> generations can still meet their own needs.

4) Maintaining <u>biodiversity</u> (see page 32) is an important part of sustainability. <u>Loss</u> of biodiversity means that future generations won't be able to get the things from the environment that we can today. For example, the <u>extinction</u> of some species could mean a reduction in our ability to <u>produce food</u> or find <u>new medicines</u>.

EXAMPLE

Large-scale <u>monoculture crop production</u> (where farmers grow fields containing only <u>one type</u> of crop) is <u>not sustainable</u> because it doesn't help to maintain biodiversity. A single type of crop will support <u>fewer species</u> than a field containing lots of different species.

Packaging Materials *can be Made* More Sustainable

<u>Packaging materials</u> are usually <u>thrown away</u>. This isn't <u>sustainable</u> because:

1) The <u>resources</u> that have gone into making the packaging material aren't (or can't be) <u>re-used</u> so they are no longer available to future generations.

2) Lots of <u>energy</u> has been used to make the packaging materials and producing energy, e.g. by burning fossil fuels, <u>damages</u> the environment.

3) Most waste is thrown into <u>landfill sites</u>, which <u>uses up space</u> and damages the environment.

The sustainability of using packaging materials can be <u>improved</u> through:

1) <u>Using renewable materials</u>: A lot of packaging materials come from <u>non-renewable</u> resources, e.g. plastic is made from oil. Using materials like <u>paper</u> and <u>card</u> (from trees) can improve sustainability as the resources can be <u>replaced</u> once they've been used, e.g. by planting more trees.

2) <u>Using less energy</u>: Making packaging from <u>recycled</u> materials uses <u>less energy</u> than producing new materials. This means the environment isn't <u>damaged</u> as much because less energy (from burning fossil fuels) is <u>required</u>.

3) <u>Creating less pollution</u>: Most plastics aren't <u>biodegradeable</u>. This means they <u>can't</u> be broken down naturally by <u>microorganisms</u>, so they will <u>pollute</u> the land for hundreds of years. Using <u>biodegradeable</u> packaging materials (e.g. wood) is <u>more sustainable</u> because they will rot away more easily.

The <u>most</u> sustainable thing to do is to <u>use less</u> packaging material. Even when <u>biodegradeable materials</u> are used, they still take <u>a while</u> to break down in landfill sites because there's <u>not much oxygen</u> available. Also, <u>making</u> and <u>transporting</u> any packaging material <u>uses up energy</u>.

This section is not sustainable — it's going to run out soon...

It's easy to dismiss all this <u>sustainability</u> stuff as tosh, but we really need to pull our socks up and think of sustainable ways of supporting <u>our needs</u>. Make sure you understand <u>what</u> sustainability is and <u>how</u> to improve it.

Revision Summary for Module B3

Well, well, well, another section down. At this rate, you'll be a fully qualified GCSE scientist. But let's not get ahead of ourselves — there's still the small matter of these questions I've laid out for you. Have a go at all of them and if there's any that you can't do, go back and have a look at the section again. When you can do them all, you can feel pretty smug that you know the section really well.

1) What is a species?
2) Name three features of a plant, animal or other organism that shows they're adapted to their habitat.
3) Which has a greater effect on a species — mutations in body cells or mutations in sex cells?
4) True or false — If an organism randomly develops a feature that gives it a survival advantage, then it will be more likely to survive than other organisms, and will also be more likely to produce offspring which also have this advantageous feature. Eventually, many organisms will have the feature.
5) How does selective breeding differ from natural selection?
6) How long ago did life begin on Earth?
7) Explain how evolution could lead to the formation of a new species.
8) How do fossils provide evidence that we evolved from simpler life forms?
9) How do scientists use DNA evidence to show evolution?
10) Give one reason why Lamarck's theory of evolution was rejected in favour of Darwin's theory.
11) What is biodiversity?
12) Give one likely cause for the increasing rate of species extinction.
13) Give one reason why scientists classify organisms.
14) Give one factor that scientists use when classifying organisms to put them into the same group.
15) Explain how the classification system can show us the evolutionary relationships between organisms.
16) List four factors that are essential for plants to live.
17) Explain why organisms have to compete for resources in their environment.
18) True or false — in a food web, if one organism dies out, the other organisms will not be affected.
19) What are the three main reasons for a species becoming extinct?
20) What is the source of all the energy in a typical ecosystem?
21) Explain how energy is transferred between plants and animals in an ecosystem.
22) Give three ways that energy is lost at each stage in the food chain.
23) Why is it unusual to find a food chain with more than five stages?
24) In the carbon cycle, how is carbon dioxide turned into carbon compounds?
25) How is carbon passed between animals in an ecosystem?
26) Give four ways that carbon returns to the air.
27) What role do decomposers play in the nitrogen cycle?
28) Which microorganisms turn ammonia into nitrates?
29) What important role do nitrogen-fixing bacteria play in the nitrogen cycle?
30) What role do denitrifying bacteria play in the nitrogen cycle?
31) Give three non-living indicators that can be used to measure environmental change.
32) Explain how mayfly nymphs can be used to measure environmental change.
33) Name two other living indicators of environmental change (other than mayfly nymphs).
34) Define sustainability.
35) What is monoculture? Explain the effect of large-scale monoculture on biodiversity.
36) Explain two ways that packaging materials can be made more sustainable.
37) Explain why decreasing the amount of packaging material used is the most sustainable solution.

Cell Structure and Function

Every living thing, from your teacher to your pet pooch, is made up of the same basic building blocks — cells. Lots of important chemical reactions happen in cells — you need to know about the different parts involved.

Plant and Animal Cells Have Similarities and Differences

Most animal and plant cells have the following parts — make sure you know them all:

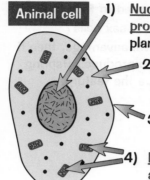

Animal cell

1) Nucleus — contains DNA (see page 49). DNA contains the instructions for making proteins, e.g. the enzymes used in the chemical reactions of respiration (in animal and plant cells, see pages 42-43) and photosynthesis (in plant cells only, see page 44).

2) Cytoplasm — gel-like substance where proteins like enzymes (see page 41) are made. Some enzyme-controlled reactions take place in the cytoplasm, e.g. the reactions of anaerobic respiration (see page 43).

3) Cell membrane — holds the cell together and controls what goes in and out. It lets gases and water pass through freely while acting as a barrier to other chemicals.

4) Mitochondria — these are where the enzymes needed for the reactions of aerobic respiration (see page 42) are found, and where the reactions take place.

Plant cells also have a few extra things that animal cells don't have:

Plant cell

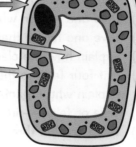

1) Rigid cell wall — made of cellulose. It supports the cell and strengthens it.

2) Vacuole — contains cell sap, a weak solution of sugar and salts.

3) Chloroplasts — these are where the reactions for photosynthesis take place. They contain a green substance called chlorophyll and the enzymes needed for photosynthesis.

Yeast are Single Celled Microorganisms

1) Yeast are used to make bread and wine (see page 43).

2) You need to learn the different parts of a yeast cell:

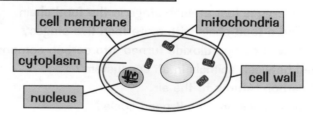

cell membrane mitochondria cytoplasm cell wall nucleus

Bacteria Have a Simple Cell Structure

1) Bacterial cells are a bit different to plant, animal and yeast cells. You need to know the different parts of a bacterial cell:

2) They don't have a nucleus. They have a circular molecule of DNA which floats around in the cytoplasm.

3) They don't have mitochondria either, but they can still respire aerobically.

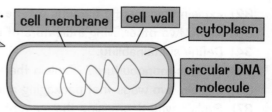

cell membrane cell wall cytoplasm circular DNA molecule

At yeast it's an easy page...

It might look like there's lots on the page but don't let that put you off — it's not as mind boggling as it seems and there's a dead simple way of learning it all. Just draw a table showing the different parts of plant, animal, yeast and bacterial cells. Then learn the table and before you know it you'll be an expert on cells just like me.

Enzymes

Without enzymes, all the <u>chemical reactions</u> taking place inside cells would run dead slowly — so your body wouldn't function properly. But enzymes won't work if they don't have the <u>right conditions</u>.

Enzymes <u>are</u> Proteins <u>Produced by</u> Living Things

1) <u>Living things</u> have thousands of different <u>chemical reactions</u> going on inside them all the time.

2) These reactions need to be <u>carefully controlled</u> — to get the <u>right</u> amounts of substances.

3) So... living things produce <u>enzymes</u>:

> <u>ENZYMES</u> are proteins that <u>SPEED UP CHEMICAL REACTIONS</u>

4) The <u>instructions</u> for making enzymes and other proteins are found in a cell's <u>genes</u> (see page 8).

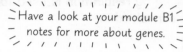
Have a look at your module B1 notes for more about genes.

Enzymes <u>are Very</u> Specific

1) <u>Chemical reactions</u> usually involve things either being <u>split apart</u> or <u>joined together</u>.

2) A <u>substrate</u> is a molecule that is <u>changed</u> in a reaction.

3) <u>Every</u> enzyme molecule has an <u>active site</u> — the part where a substrate <u>joins on</u> to the enzyme.

4) Enzymes are really <u>picky</u> — they usually only speed up <u>one reaction</u>. This is because, for an enzyme to work, a substrate has to be the <u>correct shape</u> to <u>fit</u> into the <u>active site</u>.

5) This is called the <u>'lock and key' model</u>, because the substrate fits into the enzyme just like a key fits into a lock.

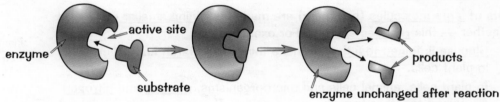
active site
enzyme
substrate
products
enzyme unchanged after reaction

Enzymes <u>Need the</u> Right Temperature <u>and</u> pH

Enzymes need to be at a <u>specific constant temperature</u> to work at their <u>optimum</u> (when they're <u>most active</u>).

1) Changing the <u>temperature</u> changes the <u>rate</u> of an enzyme-controlled reaction.

2) A higher temperature <u>increases</u> the rate at first.

3) But, if it gets <u>too hot</u>, some of the <u>bonds</u> holding the enzyme together <u>break</u>. This <u>changes</u> the shape of the enzyme's <u>active site</u> and so the substrate will <u>no longer fit</u> and the enzyme <u>won't work</u> any more. It's said to be <u>denatured</u>.

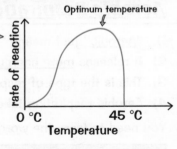
Optimum temperature
rate of reaction
0 °C   45 °C
Temperature

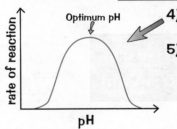
Optimum pH
rate of reaction
pH

4) All enzymes also have an <u>optimum pH</u> that they work best at.

5) If the pH is too high or too low, it interferes with the <u>bonds</u> holding the enzyme together. This changes the shape of the <u>active site</u> and <u>denatures</u> the enzyme.

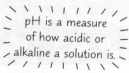
pH is a measure of how acidic or alkaline a solution is.

If only enzymes could speed up revision...

Just like you've got to have the correct key for a lock, enzymes have got to have the <u>right substrate</u>. If a substrate <u>doesn't fit</u>, the enzyme <u>won't</u> speed up the reaction...

Aerobic Respiration

Respiration doesn't sound very rock 'n' roll but it keeps you alive. The basic processes of life (e.g. movement) depend on chemical reactions. Most of these reactions are powered by the energy released by respiration.

Respiration is NOT "Breathing In and Out"

1) Respiration is NOT breathing in and breathing out, as you might think.

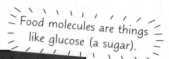
Food molecules are things like glucose (a sugar).

> RESPIRATION is a series of chemical reactions that RELEASE ENERGY by breaking down large FOOD MOLECULES. It happens in EVERY LIVING CELL.

2) The energy released by respiration is used to power some of the chemical reactions that happen in cells, e.g. the reactions involved in:

MOVEMENT

Energy is needed to make muscles contract.

ACTIVE TRANSPORT

This process uses energy to move some substances in and out of cells (see page 47 for more).

SYNTHESIS OF LARGE MOLECULES

Lots of large molecules (polymers) are made by joining smaller molecules together — this requires energy. For example:

- Glucose is joined together to make things like starch and cellulose in plant cells.
- In plant cells, animal cells and microorganisms, glucose and nitrogen are joined together to make amino acids. The amino acids are joined together to make proteins.

Plants get their nitrogen from nitrates in the soil.

3) There are two types of respiration — aerobic and anaerobic.

Aerobic Respiration Needs Plenty of Oxygen

1) "Aerobic" just means "with oxygen".
2) It releases more energy per glucose molecule than anaerobic respiration.
3) This is the type of respiration that you're using most of the time.
4) Aerobic respiration takes place in animal and plant cells, and in some microorganisms.

Anaerobic respiration is covered on the next page.

You need to learn the word equation and the symbol equation of aerobic respiration:

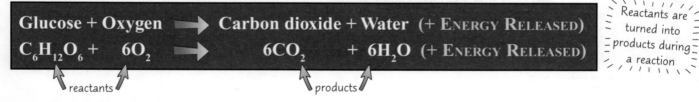

Glucose + Oxygen $\longrightarrow$ Carbon dioxide + Water (+ ENERGY RELEASED)

$$C_6H_{12}O_6 + 6O_2 \longrightarrow 6CO_2 + 6H_2O \text{ (+ ENERGY RELEASED)}$$

reactants   products

Reactants are turned into products during a reaction

Don't stop respirin' — hold on to that feelin' (of being alive)...

Isn't it strange to think that each individual living cell in your body is respiring every second of every day, releasing energy from the food you eat. Next time someone accuses you of being lazy you could claim that you're busy respiring — it's enough to make anyone feel tired.

Anaerobic Respiration

If you thought that was it for respiration, you'd be wrong. Next up, anaerobic respiration...

Anaerobic Respiration **Doesn't Use Oxygen**

1) "Anaerobic" just means "without oxygen".

2) Anaerobic respiration takes place in animal and plant cells and some microorganisms when there's very little or no oxygen. For example:

HUMAN CELLS	When you do really vigorous exercise your body can't supply enough oxygen to your muscle cells for aerobic respiration — they have to start respiring anaerobically.
PLANT CELLS	If the soil a plant's growing in becomes waterlogged there'll be no oxygen available for the roots — so the root cells will have to respire anaerobically.
BACTERIAL CELLS	Bacteria can get under your skin through puncture wounds caused by things like nails. There's very little oxygen under your skin, so only bacteria that can respire anaerobically can survive there.

3) Energy is always released during anaerobic respiration, but the products of the reactions are different depending on the type of cell it happens in.

Anaerobic Respiration **Can Produce** Lactic Acid

In animal cells and some bacteria anaerobic respiration produces lactic acid:

Glucose ⟹ Lactic Acid (+ ENERGY RELEASED)
  reactant   product

Don't forget that anaerobic respiration releases less energy per glucose molecule than aerobic respiration.

Anaerobic Respiration **Can Also Produce** Ethanol **and** Carbon Dioxide

1) In plant cells and some microorganisms (like yeast), anaerobic respiration produces ethanol and carbon dioxide:

Glucose ⟹ Ethanol + Carbon Dioxide (+ ENERGY RELEASED)
  reactant   products

2) Fermentation is when microorganisms break down sugars into other products as they respire anaerobically. Humans use fermentation to make lots of things, for example:

BIOGAS
1) Biogas is a fuel used for things like heating and lighting.
2) Lots of different microorganisms are used to produce biogas.
3) They ferment plant and animal waste, which contains carbohydrates.
4) The biogas they produce is mainly made of methane and carbon dioxide.

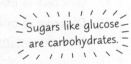

Sugars like glucose are carbohydrates.

BREAD
1) Bread is made using yeast.
2) The yeast ferment the carbohydrates in the flour and release carbon dioxide — this causes the bread to rise.

ALCOHOL
1) Yeast ferment sugar to form alcohol (ethanol).
2) The sugar used in alcohol production comes from things like grapes (which you use to make wine) and barley (which you use to make beer).

Anaerobic respiration — the best thing since sliced bread...

Anaerobic respiration is way more useful than it sounds — it's given us bread, and so more importantly, the wonder of toast. The world would be a very sad place without toast — there'd be nothing to put your beans on...

Photosynthesis

Some organisms <u>make</u> their <u>own food</u>. It's not restaurant-quality grub, but you need to know <u>how</u> it's done.

Photosynthesis **Produces** Glucose

1) Predictable I know, but first of all you need to know this <u>definition</u> of <u>photosynthesis</u>:

> <u>PHOTOSYNTHESIS</u> is a series of chemical reactions that <u>USES ENERGY</u> from <u>SUNLIGHT</u> to <u>PRODUCE FOOD</u>.

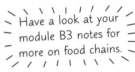

2) The 'food' it produces is <u>glucose</u> — a <u>sugar</u>.

3) Photosynthesis happens in:
   - The <u>cells</u> in <u>green parts</u> of <u>plants</u>, e.g. leaf cells.
   - Some microorganisms, e.g. <u>phytoplankton</u>.

4) <u>Chlorophyll</u> is needed for photosynthesis to happen.

5) It's a <u>green substance</u> which absorbs <u>sunlight</u> and allows the energy to be used to convert <u>carbon dioxide</u> (CO_2) and <u>water</u> into <u>glucose</u>.

6) <u>Oxygen</u> is produced as a <u>waste product</u> of photosynthesis. Here are the equations:

> carbon dioxide + water $\xrightarrow{\text{LIGHT ENERGY}}$ glucose + oxygen
>
> $6CO_2$ + $6H_2O$ $\longrightarrow$ $C_6H_{12}O_6$ + $6O_2$

reactants   products

7) Organisms that photosynthesise form the <u>start</u> of <u>food chains</u>. They make the <u>energy</u> from the Sun <u>available</u> to other organisms by converting it to glucose. The energy is <u>transferred</u> when the photosynthetic organisms are <u>eaten</u>.

Have a look at your module B3 notes for more on food chains.

Plants Use the Glucose in Three **Main Ways**

(1) ### Glucose is Used for Respiration

1) Plants use some of the glucose for <u>respiration</u> (see pages 42-43).
2) This process <u>releases energy</u> from the glucose.

(2) ### Glucose is Used to Make Chemicals **for** Growth

1) Glucose is converted into <u>cellulose</u> for making <u>cell walls</u>, especially in a rapidly growing plant.
2) Glucose is combined with <u>nitrogen</u> (from nitrates taken up from the soil by plant roots) to make <u>amino acids</u>, which are then made into <u>proteins</u>.
3) Glucose is also used to help make <u>chlorophyll</u>.

(3) ### Glucose is Stored as Starch

<u>Glucose</u> is turned into <u>starch</u> and <u>stored</u> in roots, stems and leaves. It's used at times when the rate of photosynthesis is slower, like in the <u>winter</u>.

Convert this page into stored information...

Without plants we'd all be pretty stuffed really — plants are able to use the Sun's energy to <u>make glucose</u>. This is the <u>energy source</u> which humans and all other animals need for <u>respiration</u>.

Rate of Photosynthesis

The rate of photosynthesis is affected by environmental conditions...

Three Factors Affect the Rate of Photosynthesis

1) There are three factors that can affect the rate of photosynthesis...

> 1) amount of <u>light</u>
> 2) amount of <u>CO₂</u>
> 3) <u>temperature</u>

2) Any of these three factors can become the <u>limiting factor</u>. This just means that it <u>stops</u> photosynthesis from <u>happening any faster</u>.

Plants also need water but if water is so low that it becomes the limiting factor, the plant's probably already nearly dead.

3) Which factor is limiting at a particular time depends on the <u>environmental conditions</u>:
- at <u>night</u> it's pretty obvious that <u>light</u> is the limiting factor,
- in <u>winter</u> it's often the <u>temperature</u>,
- if it's warm enough and bright enough, the amount of <u>CO₂</u> is usually limiting.

Three Important Graphs for Rate of Photosynthesis

1) Not Enough Light Slows Down the Rate of Photosynthesis

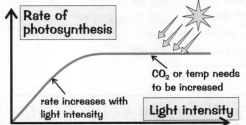

1) Light provides the <u>energy</u> needed for photosynthesis.
2) As the <u>light level</u> is raised, the rate of photosynthesis <u>increases steadily</u> — but only up to a <u>certain point</u>.
3) Beyond that, it <u>won't</u> make any difference because then it'll be either the <u>temperature</u> or the <u>CO₂ level</u> which is the limiting factor.

2) Too Little Carbon Dioxide Also Slows It Down

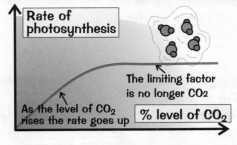

1) CO₂ is one of the <u>raw materials</u> needed for photosynthesis.
2) As with light intensity, the amount of <u>CO₂</u> will only increase the rate of photosynthesis up to a point. After this the graph <u>flattens out</u>, showing that CO₂ is no longer the <u>limiting factor</u>.
3) As long as <u>light</u> and <u>CO₂</u> are in plentiful supply then the factor limiting photosynthesis must be <u>temperature</u>.

3) The Temperature Has to be Just Right

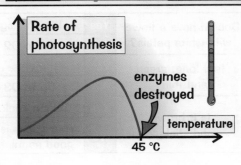

1) Usually, if the temperature is the <u>limiting factor</u> it's because it's <u>too low</u> — the <u>enzymes</u> (see page 41) needed for photosynthesis work more <u>slowly</u> at low temperatures.
2) But if the plant gets <u>too hot</u>, the enzymes it needs for photosynthesis and its other reactions will be <u>denatured</u>.
3) This happens at about <u>45 °C</u> (which is pretty hot for outdoors, although <u>greenhouses</u> can get that hot if you're not careful).

Don't blame it on the sunshine, don't blame it on the CO₂...

...don't blame it on the temperature, blame it on the plant. You might get asked to <u>interpret data</u> on factors that <u>limit</u> the <u>rate of photosynthesis</u> in the exam, so get the info on this page burned into your brain.

Investigating Photosynthesis

You need to know about how to <u>investigate</u> the <u>effect of light</u> on <u>plants</u>. That <u>doesn't</u> mean you have to dash out and do an investigation right now — you just need to make sure you <u>know this page</u> inside out so you can <u>describe</u> how to do it. Imaginary fieldwork is almost as fun as the real thing...

You Need to Know How to *Take a Transect*

1) <u>Transects</u> are a way of <u>investigating</u> how something <u>changes across an area</u>.

2) To <u>set up</u> a transect you just run a <u>tape measure</u> between <u>two fixed points</u>.

3) Then all you do is <u>start</u> at <u>one end</u> of the transect and <u>collect</u> the <u>data</u> you want.

4) Then <u>move</u> along the transect and <u>collect</u> the <u>data</u> again.

5) You just <u>keep collecting</u> data and <u>moving</u> until you reach the <u>end</u> of the transect.

tape measure

For example, if you were investigating the <u>effect of light</u> on the <u>distribution</u> of <u>plant species</u> you could take a transect across an area where the <u>light level changes</u> (e.g. from woodland into an open field). You could collect data on how the <u>percentage cover</u> (see below) of different species <u>changes</u> across the transect.

You Need to Know About Some Things That'll Help You *Collect Data*

You need to know about a few other things that are <u>pretty useful</u> for investigating the effect of light on plants:

LIGHT METER
You'd need to <u>measure</u> the <u>level of light</u>, e.g. if you were comparing plants in areas with different levels of light. You could use a <u>LIGHT METER</u> to do this — it's a <u>sensor</u> that <u>accurately</u> measures light level.

QUADRAT
To make data collection <u>quicker</u> and <u>easier</u> you could use a <u>QUADRAT</u> (a <u>square frame</u> divided into a <u>grid</u> of 100 smaller squares). For example, you can <u>estimate</u> the <u>percentage cover</u> of a plant species on the ground by counting <u>how much</u> of the quadrat is <u>covered</u> by the <u>species</u> — you count a square if it's more than half-covered.

IDENTIFICATION KEY
To identify the different plant species you're looking at you could use an <u>IDENTIFICATION KEY</u>. It's a <u>series of questions</u> that you can use to figure out what a plant is. You start at question 1 and the answer is used to <u>narrow down</u> your options of what the plant could be. As you answer more and more questions you're eventually just <u>left with one</u> possible species your plant could be.

Q1	Does it have a flower with white petals?	Yes	It's a daisy.
		No	Go to Q2
Q2	Is it long, green and thin?	Yes	It's grass.
		No	Go to Q3
Q3	Is it brown and sticky?	Yes	It's a stick.
		No	Your guess is as good as mine...

Is it never-ending and the least fun ever? Yes — it's revising for exams...

I think you'll agree that this has been the <u>most exciting</u> page in the book so far... Luckily this stuff is <u>pretty</u> <u>straightforward</u> — just learn the page until all this information has lodged itself in your brain box.

Diffusion, Osmosis and Active Transport

Cells are pretty fussy — the levels of certain substances need to be controlled in order for them to function properly. These substances move in and out of cells in three main ways that you need to know about...

Diffusion — Don't be Put Off by the Fancy Word

"Diffusion" is simple. It's just the gradual movement of particles from places where there are lots of them to places where there are fewer of them. That's all it is — just the natural tendency for stuff to spread out. Unfortunately you also have to learn the fancy way of saying the same thing, which is this:

> **DIFFUSION** is the *passive overall movement* of *particles* from a region of their **HIGHER CONCENTRATION** to a region of their **LOWER CONCENTRATION**.

'Passive' just means that it takes place without needing any energy.

Here's an example — when plants photosynthesise they use up CO_2 from the atmosphere and produce O_2 (see page 44). These gases pass in and out of plant leaves by diffusion.

Osmosis is a Specific Case of Diffusion, That's All

Osmosis is a type of diffusion — the passive movement of water molecules from an area of higher concentration to an area of lower concentration.

> *Osmosis* is the overall *movement of water* from a **DILUTE** to a **MORE CONCENTRATED** solution through a *partially permeable membrane*.

A dilute solution has a higher concentration of water molecules than a concentrated solution.

1) A partially permeable membrane is just one that only allows certain substances to diffuse through it. For example, it may only allow small molecules like water to pass through and not larger molecules like sucrose.

2) This concentrated sucrose solution gets more dilute as more water moves in. The water acts like it's trying to even up the concentration either side of the membrane.

3) Plants take in water by osmosis. There's usually a higher concentration of water in the soil than there is inside the plant, so the water is drawn into the root by osmosis.

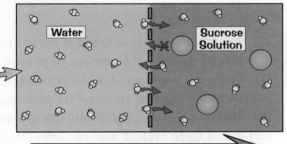

Water | Sucrose Solution

Net movement of water molecules

Some Chemicals can be Moved by Active Transport

Sometimes chemicals, e.g. glucose, need to be moved from an area with a lower concentration of the chemical to an area with a higher concentration across a cell membrane. This is done by a process called active transport — it uses energy from respiration (see page 42).

> *Active transport* is the overall *movement of chemicals* across a *cell membrane* from a region of **LOWER CONCENTRATION** to a region of **HIGHER CONCENTRATION** using **ENERGY** released by respiration.

Here's an example — plants take in minerals like nitrates through their roots by active transport. The concentration of minerals in root cells is normally higher than in the soil around them. Active transport uses energy from respiration to move minerals from the soil into the root cells.

Revision by diffusion — you wish...

Wouldn't that be great — if all the ideas in this book would just gradually drift across into your mind, from an area of high concentration (in the book) to an area of low concentration (in your mind — no offence). Actually, that will probably happen if you read it again. Why don't you give it a go...

Revision Summary for Module B4

Now it's time to find out if you know your stuff. Have a bash at the questions, go back and check anything you're not sure about, then try again. Practise until you can answer all these questions really easily without having to look back at the section. I know you want to look at the section again, right now, as it is so exciting and so beautifully made. But you can't — not until you've had a go at these equally thrilling questions...

1) What is the function of:
   a) the nucleus
   b) the cytoplasm
   c) the cell membrane
   d) mitochondria
2) Name three things that plant cells have and animal cells don't.
3) Yeast cells have mitochondria and a nucleus. True or false?
4) What type of cells have a cell wall but no nucleus?
5) Give a definition of an enzyme.
6) Describe the 'lock and key' model.
7) Name two things that affect how quickly an enzyme works.
8) What is a denatured enzyme?
9) Name three things that the energy released by respiration is used for.
10) What type of respiration, aerobic or anaerobic, releases more energy per glucose molecule?
11) Write the word equation for aerobic respiration.
12) Write the symbol equation for aerobic respiration.
13) Give an example of when human cells respire anaerobically.
14) Anaerobic respiration releases energy. What else does it produce in:
    a) animal cells
    b) yeast cells
15) Briefly describe how bread is made using yeast.
16) Briefly describe the process of photosynthesis.
17) Write the word equation for photosynthesis.
18) Write the symbol equation for photosynthesis.
19) Give three main ways plants use glucose.
20) Name three factors that can limit the rate of photosynthesis.
21) Describe how to take a transect.
22) Describe how you might use a quadrat when investigating plants.
23) What is an identification key?
24) Give a definition of diffusion.
25) Give two examples of chemicals that can move in or out of leaf cells by diffusion.
26) What is osmosis?
27) Give two ways in which active transport differs from diffusion.

DNA — Making Proteins

This module's about <u>growth and development</u> in plants and animals, including you. All the instructions for how to grow and develop are contained in your <u>DNA</u>. DNA molecules contain a <u>genetic code</u>, which is basically a long list of instructions for how to make <u>all the proteins</u> in your body.

DNA *is a Double Helix of Paired Bases*

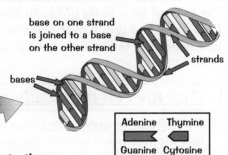

base on one strand is joined to a base on the other strand

strands

bases

Adenine Thymine

Guanine Cytosine

1) A DNA molecule has <u>two strands</u> coiled together in the shape of a <u>double helix</u> (two spirals).

2) Each strand is made up of lots of small units called <u>nucleotides</u>.

3) Each <u>nucleotide</u> contains a small molecule called a <u>base</u>. DNA has just <u>four</u> different bases — <u>adenine</u> (A), <u>cytosine</u> (C), <u>guanine</u> (G) and <u>thymine</u> (T).

4) The two strands are <u>held together</u> by the bases, which always <u>pair up</u> in the same way — it's always A-T and C-G. This is called <u>base pairing</u>.

DNA *Controls the Production of Proteins in a Cell*

1) A <u>gene</u> is a <u>section of DNA</u> that contains the instructions for <u>one</u> particular <u>protein</u>.

2) Cells make <u>proteins</u> by joining <u>amino acids</u> together in a particular order.

3) It's the order of the <u>bases</u> in a gene that <u>tells the cell</u> in what order to put the <u>amino acids</u> together.

4) Each set of <u>three bases</u> (called a <u>triplet</u>) <u>codes</u> for one <u>amino acid</u>.

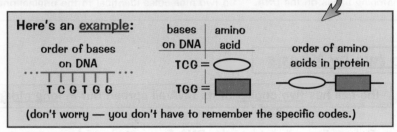

Here's an <u>example</u>:

order of bases on DNA

· · · | | | | | | · · ·
 T C G T G G

bases on DNA	amino acid
TCG =	(ellipse)
TGG =	(rectangle)

order of amino acids in protein

(don't worry — you don't have to remember the specific codes.)

Proteins *are Made by Ribosomes*

Proteins are made in the cell <u>cytoplasm</u> by <u>organelles</u> called <u>ribosomes</u>. DNA is found in the cell <u>nucleus</u> and can't move out of it because it's really big. To get the information from the DNA to the ribosome, a <u>copy</u> of the DNA is made using a molecule called <u>messenger RNA</u>. Messenger RNA is very similar to DNA but it's much shorter and only a single strand. Here's how it's done:

Organelles are parts of cells, e.g. nucleus, chloroplasts.

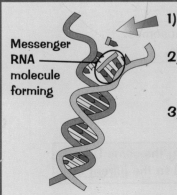

Messenger RNA molecule forming

1) The two DNA strands <u>unzip</u>. A molecule of <u>messenger RNA</u> is made using one strand of the DNA as a <u>template</u>. Base pairing ensures it's an exact match.

2) The messenger RNA molecule <u>moves out</u> of the nucleus and <u>joins</u> with a ribosome in the cytoplasm.

3) The job of the ribosome is to <u>stick amino acids together</u> in a chain to make a <u>protein</u>, following the order of bases in the messenger RNA.

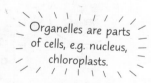

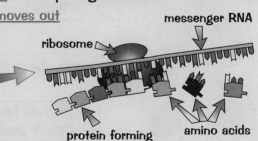

messenger RNA

ribosome

protein forming

amino acids

What do DNA and a game of rounders have in common?

...they both have four bases. Genes <u>control</u> what <u>proteins</u> are made. And proteins are essential things — all your body's enzymes are proteins and enzymes control the making of your other, non-protein bits.

Cell Division — Mitosis

Your cells have to be able to <u>divide</u> for your body to <u>grow</u>. And that means your <u>DNA</u> has to be copied...

New Cells are Needed for Growth and Repair

The cells of your body <u>divide</u> to <u>produce more cells</u>, so your body can <u>grow</u> and <u>replace</u> damaged cells.
Cells <u>grow</u> and <u>divide</u> over and over again — this is called the <u>cell cycle</u>. Of course, cell division doesn't
just happen in humans — animals and plants do it too. There are two stages...

First the cell physically grows and duplicates its contents...

The cell has to <u>copy everything</u> it contains so that when it <u>splits</u> in
half the two new cells will contain the right amount of material.

1) The <u>number</u> of <u>organelles increases</u> during cell growth.

2) The <u>chromosomes</u> are <u>copied</u>, so that the cell has <u>two copies</u> of its DNA:

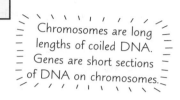

Chromosomes are long
lengths of coiled DNA.
Genes are short sections
of DNA on chromosomes.

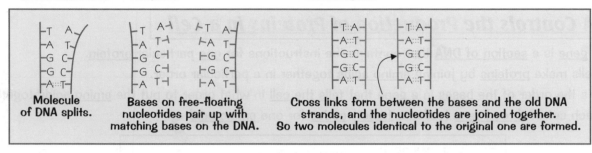

Molecule
of DNA splits.

Bases on free-floating
nucleotides pair up with
matching bases on the DNA.

Cross links form between the bases and the old DNA
strands, and the nucleotides are joined together.
So two molecules identical to the original one are formed.

...then it splits into two by Mitosis

The cell has <u>two copies</u> of its DNA all spread out in <u>long strings</u>.

Before the cell <u>divides</u>, the DNA forms <u>X-shaped</u>
chromosomes. Each 'arm' of a chromosome is an
<u>exact duplicate</u> of the other.

The left arm has
the same DNA as
the right arm of
the chromosome.

The chromosomes then <u>line up</u> at the centre of the
cell and <u>cell fibres</u> pull them apart. The <u>two arms</u> of
each chromosome go to <u>opposite ends</u> of the cell.

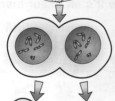

<u>Membranes</u> form around each of the sets of chromosomes.
These become the <u>nuclei</u> of the two new cells.

Lastly, the <u>cytoplasm</u> divides.

You now have <u>two new cells</u> containing exactly the same DNA
— they're <u>genetically identical</u> to <u>each other</u> and to the <u>parent cell</u>.

A cell's favourite computer game — divide and conquer...

This can seem tricky at first. But don't worry — just go through it <u>slowly</u>, one step at a time.
This type of division produces <u>genetically identical</u> cells, but there's another type which doesn't... (see next page)

Cell Division — Meiosis

All the cells in your body divide by mitosis <u>except</u> cells in your reproductive organs — they divide by <u>meiosis</u> to form sperm or egg cells (<u>gametes</u>).

Gametes <u>Have</u> Half <u>the Usual Number of</u> Chromosomes

1) During <u>sexual reproduction</u>, an egg and a sperm combine to form a new cell, called a <u>zygote</u>.

2) All human body cells have <u>two copies</u> of the 23 chromosomes (so <u>46 in total</u>). But gametes only have <u>one copy</u> of each chromosome (<u>23 in total</u>).

3) So when the egg and sperm combine the zygote will contain <u>46 chromosomes</u> — one <u>set of 23</u> from <u>each parent</u>.

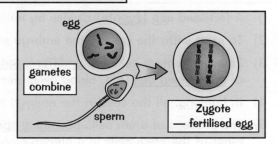

Gametes <u>are Produced by</u> Meiosis

Meiosis involves <u>TWO divisions</u>. It produces new cells that only have <u>half</u> the original number of chromosomes. In humans it <u>only</u> happens in the ovaries and testes (reproductive organs).

> "MEIOSIS produces cells which have HALF the normal number of chromosomes."

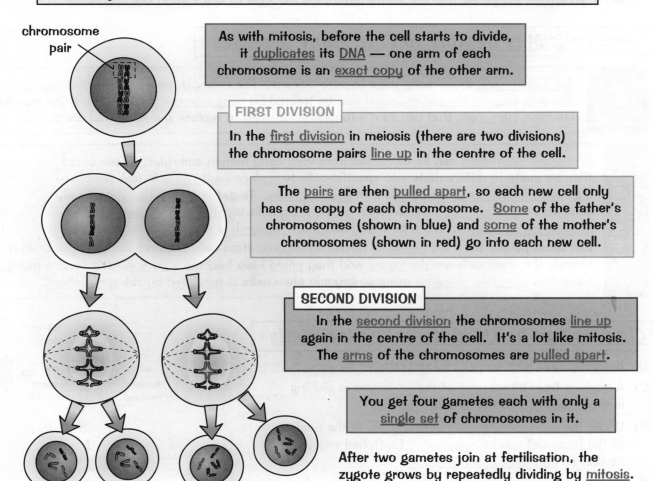

chromosome pair

As with mitosis, before the cell starts to divide, it <u>duplicates</u> its <u>DNA</u> — one arm of each chromosome is an <u>exact copy</u> of the other arm.

FIRST DIVISION

In the <u>first division</u> in meiosis (there are two divisions) the chromosome pairs <u>line up</u> in the centre of the cell.

The <u>pairs</u> are then <u>pulled apart</u>, so each new cell only has one copy of each chromosome. <u>Some</u> of the father's chromosomes (shown in blue) and <u>some</u> of the mother's chromosomes (shown in red) go into each new cell.

SECOND DIVISION

In the <u>second division</u> the chromosomes <u>line up</u> again in the centre of the cell. It's a lot like mitosis. The <u>arms</u> of the chromosomes are <u>pulled apart</u>.

You get four gametes each with only a <u>single set</u> of chromosomes in it.

After two gametes join at fertilisation, the zygote grows by repeatedly dividing by <u>mitosis</u>.

Now that I have your undivided attention...

Remember — in humans, meiosis only occurs in <u>reproductive organs</u>, where gametes are being made.

Animal Development

Every living organism is made up of cells. Multicellular organisms are organisms that have lots of cells — most of their cells are specialised to do a particular job, e.g. carry oxygen around the body.

Cells in an Early Embryo Can Turn into Any Type of Cell

1) A fertilised egg (zygote) divides by mitosis to produce a bundle of cells — the embryo of the new organism.

2) To start with, the cells in the embryo are all the same. They're called embryonic stem cells.

3) Embryonic stem cells are undifferentiated. This means they're able to divide to produce any type of specialised cell (e.g. blood cells, nerve cells).

4) In humans, all the cells in the embryo are undifferentiated up to the eight cell stage.

5) The process of stem cells becoming specialised is called differentiation. After the eight cell stage, most of the stem cells in a human embryo start to differentiate. The embryo then begins to develop tissues (groups of specialised cells) and organs (groups of tissues).

6) Adult humans only have stem cells in certain places like the bone marrow. Adult stem cells can become specialised but they aren't as versatile as embryonic stem cells — they can only differentiate into certain types of cell.

Have a look at your module B1 notes for more on stem cells.

7) All body cells contain the same genes, but in specialised cells most of the genes are not active — they only produce the specific proteins they need. Stem cells can switch on any gene during their development — the genes that are active determine the type of cell a stem cell specialises into.

Stem Cells May be Able to Cure Many Diseases

ADULT STEM CELLS

Adult stem cells are already used to cure disease. For example, people with some blood diseases (e.g. sickle-cell anaemia) can be treated by bone marrow transplants. Bone marrow contains stem cells that can turn into new blood cells to replace the faulty old ones.

EMBRYONIC STEM CELLS

Embryonic stem cells can be extracted from very early human embryos. These could then be made to differentiate into specific cells to replace faulty cells in sick people — e.g. heart muscle cells for people with heart disease. To get one specific type of cell, scientists try to control differentiation of the stem cells by altering the conditions to activate certain genes. It's a bit tricky and more research is needed.

But some people think it's unethical to use embryonic stem cells because the embryos used to provide the stem cells are destroyed and they could have become a person. It's such a tricky issue that scientific research using embryonic stem cells is regulated by the government.

Cloning Can be Used to Make Stem Cells

1) Basically, you take an egg cell and remove its genetic material.

2) A nucleus from a body cell of the adult you're cloning is then inserted into the 'empty' egg cell.

3) Under the right conditions, inactive genes in the nucleus of the body cell can be reactivated (switched on) so that an embryo forms.

4) Embryonic stem cells can then be extracted from the embryo — these stem cells could then be controlled to form any type of specialised cell.

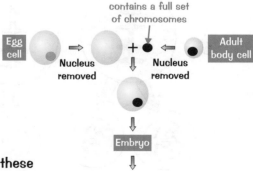

Develop — birds do it, bees do it, even educated fleas do it...

Stem cell research is a controversial issue, but you need to know what stem cells are and what they could be used for — not just to impress your friends, but because it might come up in your exam too. So learn this page.

Plant Development

Plants, like animals, have stem cells. Yep, you guessed it, you need to know all about them too...

Meristems Contain Plant Stem Cells

1) In plants, the only cells that are mitotically active (i.e. divide by mitosis) are found in plant tissues called meristems.

2) Meristem tissue is found in the areas of a plant that are growing — such as the roots and shoots.

3) Meristems produce unspecialised cells that are able to divide and form any cell type in the plant — they act like embryonic stem cells. But unlike human stem cells, these cells can divide to generate any type of cell for as long as the plant lives.

4) The unspecialised cells can become specialised and form tissues like xylem and phloem (the water and food transport tissues).

5) These tissues can group together to form organs like leaves, roots, stems and flowers.

Clones of Plants Can be Produced from Cuttings

1) A cutting is part of a plant that has been cut off it.

2) Cuttings taken from an area of the plant that's growing will contain unspecialised meristem cells which can differentiate to make any cell.

3) This means a whole new plant can grow from the cutting which will be a clone of the parent plant.

4) Gardeners often take cuttings from parent plants with desirable characteristics, and then plant them to produce identical copies of the parent plant.

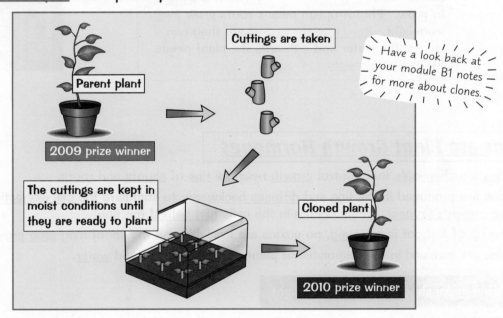

Cuttings are taken

Parent plant

2009 prize winner

Have a look back at your module B1 notes for more about clones.

The cuttings are kept in moist conditions until they are ready to plant

Cloned plant

2010 prize winner

Rooting Powder Helps Cuttings to Grow into Complete Plants

1) If you stick cuttings in the soil they won't always grow.

2) If you add rooting powder, which contains plant hormones (auxins, see next page) they'll produce roots rapidly and start growing as new plants.

3) This helps growers to produce lots of clones of a really good plant very quickly.

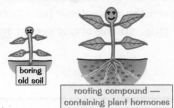

boring old soil

rooting compound — containing plant hormones

Cheery cells those Merry-stems...

So some plant cells can make any cell in the plant and for the whole time that the plant is alive. Nice.

Phototropism and Auxins

Unlike us humans, plants can't just get up and walk to something that they want. They can <u>grow</u> towards things though — <u>plant hormones</u> make sure they grow in a <u>useful direction</u> (e.g. toward light).

Phototropism __is__ Growth Towards _or_ Away __From__ Light

1) Some parts of a plant, e.g. roots and shoots, can <u>respond</u> to <u>light</u> by <u>growing</u> in a certain <u>direction</u> — this is called <u>phototropism</u>.

2) Shoots are <u>positively phototropic</u> — they grow <u>towards</u> light.

3) Roots are <u>negatively phototropic</u> — they grow <u>away</u> from light.

4) Phototropism helps plants to <u>survive</u>:

Positive Phototropism

Plants need <u>sunlight</u> for <u>photosynthesis</u>. Without sunlight, plants can't photosynthesise and don't produce the food they need for <u>energy and growth</u>. Photosynthesis occurs <u>mainly</u> in the <u>leaves</u>, so it's important for plant shoots, which will grow leaves, to grow <u>towards light</u>.

Negative Phototropism

Plants need <u>nutrients and water</u> from the <u>soil</u> to grow. Phototropism means roots grow <u>away</u> from light, <u>down into the soil</u> where they can <u>absorb</u> the water and nutrients the plant needs for <u>healthy growth</u>.

Oooh, give us a kiss...

Leave us alone!

Auxins __are Plant__ Growth Hormones

1) <u>Auxins</u> are <u>chemicals</u> that control <u>growth</u> near the <u>tips</u> of <u>shoots</u> and <u>roots</u>.

2) Auxins are produced in the <u>tips</u> and <u>diffuses backwards</u> to stimulate the <u>cell elongation (enlargement) process</u>, which occurs in the cells <u>just behind</u> the tips.

3) If the tip of a shoot is <u>removed</u>, no auxins are available and the shoot may <u>stop growing</u>.

4) Auxins are involved in the responses of plants to <u>light</u>, <u>gravity</u> and <u>water</u>.

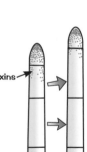

Auxins

Auxins make shoots grow towards light

1) When a <u>shoot tip</u> is exposed to <u>light</u>, <u>more auxins</u> accumulate on the side that's in the <u>shade</u> than the side that's in the light.

2) This makes the cells grow (elongate) <u>faster</u> on the <u>shaded side</u>, so the shoot grows <u>towards</u> the light.

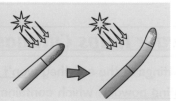

A plant auxin to a bar — 'ouch'...

<u>Phototropism</u> might not sound like the most exciting thing in the world, but it's pretty nifty stuff. If a plant grows towards <u>light</u> it can <u>photosynthesise</u> more — this means it can produce lots of <u>food</u> and <u>grow</u> quickly. A bigger plant is <u>better able</u> to <u>compete</u> with the other plants around it for resources, so it's more likely to <u>survive</u>.

Revision Summary for Module B5

Well done — you've finished another module. And what an incredibly tricky module it was — especially all the ins and outs of mitosis and meiosis. Award yourself a gold star, relax, get a cup of tea, and take a leisurely glance through these beautiful revision summary questions. Once you've glanced through them, you'll have to answer them. And then you'll have to check your answers and go back and revise any bits you got wrong. And then do the questions again. In fact, it's not really a matter of relaxing at all. More a matter of knuckling down to lots of hard work. Oops. Sorry.

1) How many different bases does DNA have?
2) Which bases always pair together?
3) What is a gene?
4) What are proteins made of?
5) Describe how the order of bases in a gene determines what protein is made.
6) Where in the cell are genes found?
7) Where in the cell are proteins made?
8) What is messenger RNA used for?
9) During cell growth does the number of chromosomes double or halve?
10)* The table below compares mitosis and meiosis. Complete the table using crosses (X) and ticks (✓) to show whether the statements are true for mitosis or meiosis. The first row's been filled in for you.

	Mitosis	Meiosis
Its purpose is to provide new cells for growth and repair.	✓	X
Its purpose is to create gametes (sex cells).		
The cells produced are genetically identical.		
The cells produced contain half the number of chromosomes that were in the parent cell.		

11) What is the name of the cell produced when two gametes combine?
12) In a human embryo, all the cells are undifferentiated until what stage?
13) How are the stem cells in an embryo different from the stem cells in an adult?
14) What determines the type of cell a stem cell becomes?
15) Describe how cloning could be used to make embryonic stem cells.
16) What name is given to the parts of plants where mitotically active cells are found?
17) Name two types of tissue that the unspecialised cells in plants can turn into.
18) What is a cutting?
19) What do cuttings grow into?
20) Why are cuttings useful?
21) What can be added to soil to encourage cuttings to grow roots?
22) What is phototropism?
23) Are shoots negatively or positively phototropic?
24) Explain how auxins cause plant shoots to grow towards light.

* Answers on page 84.

The Nervous System

The environment around you is <u>constantly changing</u>. A <u>change</u> in the <u>environment</u> of an organism is called a <u>stimulus</u>. Organisms need to <u>respond to stimuli</u> in order to <u>survive</u>. A <u>single cell</u> organism can just <u>respond</u> to its environment, but the cells of <u>multicellular</u> organisms need to <u>communicate</u> with each other so the <u>organism</u> can <u>respond</u> to stimuli. So as multicellular organisms evolved they developed <u>nervous</u> and <u>hormonal communication systems</u>.

The Nervous System Detects and Reacts to Stimuli

The Nervous System is made up of Different Parts

Central Nervous System (CNS)

In <u>vertebrates</u> (animals with backbones) this consists of the <u>brain</u> and <u>spinal cord</u> only. In <u>mammals</u>, the CNS is connected to the body by <u>sensory neurones</u> and <u>motor neurones</u> — these make up the <u>peripheral nervous system (PNS)</u>.

Sensory Neurones

The <u>neurones</u> that carry impulses from the <u>receptors</u> to the CNS.

Motor Neurones

The <u>neurones</u> that carry impulses from the CNS to <u>effectors</u>.

Effectors

All your <u>muscles</u> and <u>glands</u>, which respond to nervous impulses.

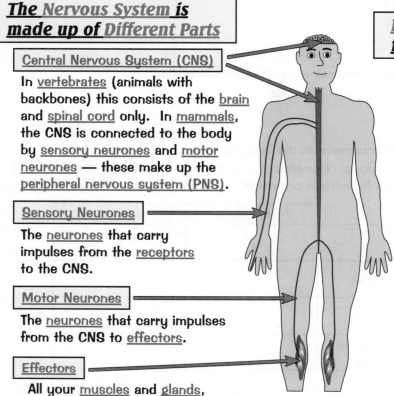

Receptors and Effectors can form part of Complex Organs

1) <u>Receptors</u> are the cells that <u>detect stimuli</u>.

2) There are many <u>different types</u> of receptors, such as <u>taste</u> receptors on the tongue and <u>sound</u> receptors in the ears.

3) Receptors can form part of <u>larger</u>, <u>complex organs</u>, e.g. the <u>retina</u> of the <u>eye</u> is covered in <u>light receptor cells</u>.

4) <u>Effectors respond</u> to nervous impulses and bring about a change. Effectors can also form part of <u>complex organs</u>.

5) There are <u>two</u> types of effector. <u>Muscle cells</u> — which make up <u>muscles</u>. And <u>hormone secreting cells</u> — which are found in <u>glands</u>, e.g. cells that secrete the <u>hormone ADH</u> are found in the <u>pituitary gland</u> (see page 27).

The Central Nervous System (CNS) Coordinates the Response

The CNS is a <u>processing centre</u> — it receives information from the <u>receptors</u> and then <u>coordinates a response</u> (decides what to do about it).

...for example, a small bird is eating some seed...

1) When, out of the corner of its eye, it spots a cat skulking towards it (this is the <u>stimulus</u>).

2) The <u>receptors</u> in the bird's eye are <u>stimulated</u>. <u>Sensory neurones</u> carry the information <u>from</u> the <u>receptors</u> to the <u>CNS</u>.

3) The CNS <u>decides</u> what to do about it.

Stimulus	Receptor	Sensory neurone	CNS	Motor neurone	Effector	Response

4) The CNS sends information to the muscles in the bird's wings (the <u>effectors</u>) along <u>motor neurones</u>. The muscles contract and the bird flies away to safety.

Light receptors in the retina

Don't let the thought of exams play on your nerves...

Don't forget that it's only large animals like mammals and birds that have <u>complex nervous systems</u>. Simple animals like jellyfish don't — everything they do is a reflex response (see page 58).

Neurones and Synapses

Neurones are nerve cells. There are a few different types but they work together to connect up the nervous system and link receptor cells (e.g. in the ears, eyes and skin) to effector cells (e.g. in muscles and glands).

Information is Transmitted Around the Body by Neurones

When stimulated, neurones transmit information around the body as electrical impulses.

1) The electrical impulses pass along the axon of the nerve cells.

2) Axons are made from the nerve cell's cytoplasm stretched out into a long fibre and surrounded by a cell membrane.

3) Some axons are also surrounded by a fatty sheath that acts as an electrical insulator, shielding the neurone from neighbouring cells and speeding up the electrical impulse.

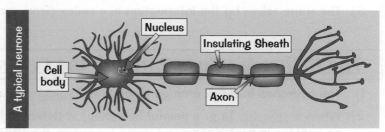

Electrical impulses carry information around the body really quickly so the responses they cause happen fast, but they're short-lived, e.g. if your hand touches something hot you pull it away and the response is over.

Hormones (e.g. insulin and oestrogen) are also used to carry information around the body — they're produced in glands and travel around in the blood. The responses they cause are brought about more slowly and they're longer lasting than the responses caused by nerve impulses.

The Gap Between Two Neurones is Called a Synapse

There are billions of neurones in the body, which connect up to form pathways. Neurones aren't attached to each other though — there's a tiny gap between them called the synapse. Information in one neurone needs to be transmitted across the synapse to the next neurone. This is done using transmitter chemicals:

1) When an electrical impulse reaches the end of a neurone it triggers the release of transmitter chemicals into the synapse.

2) The transmitter chemicals diffuse across the gap and bind to receptor molecules on the membrane of the next neurone.

3) Only specific transmitter chemicals can bind to the receptor molecules on the neurone.

4) When the chemicals bind to the right receptors they trigger a new electrical impulse in the next neurone.

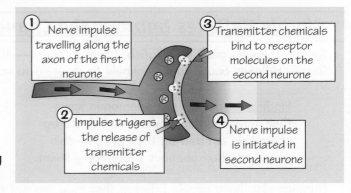

Some Drugs Affect Transmission Across Synapses

Many drugs (like ecstasy, beta-blockers and PROZAC®) and toxins can interfere with the transmission of impulses across a synapse. For example:

1) One way in which the drug ecstasy (also known as MDMA) works is to block sites in the brain's synapses where the transmitter chemical serotonin is removed.

2) Serotonin is thought to affect things like pain, aggression and appetite. It's also thought to play a large role in determining a person's mood.

3) Because the serotonin can't be removed the concentration increases — which affects a person's mood.

4) Ecstasy is often described as having mood-enhancing effects because of the increased concentrations of serotonin it causes.

Neurones transmit information from this book to your brain...

Ecstasy may make some people who take it feel happy but it's not without risks and the long-term side effects aren't fully understood. I think you'll feel happy if you learn this page from top to bottom — yes, I'm sure of it...

Reflexes

Sometimes waiting for your brain to make a decision is <u>too slow</u> — that's why you're <u>born</u> with <u>reflexes</u>. And if you're a simple animal without a brain, reflexes are pretty much all you can rely on.

Reflexes <u>are</u> Involuntary Responses

1) <u>Reflexes</u> are <u>rapid</u>, <u>automatic</u> responses to certain stimuli.

2) Reflexes are <u>quick</u> because you <u>don't think</u> about them — they're <u>involuntary</u>.

3) The route taken by the information in a reflex (from receptor to effector) is called a <u>reflex arc</u>.

The Reflex Arc <u>Goes</u> Through <u>the</u> Central Nervous System

1) The neurones in reflex arcs go through the <u>spinal cord</u> or through an <u>unconscious part of the brain</u>.

2) When a <u>stimulus</u> (e.g. a painful bee sting) is detected by receptors, an impulse is sent along a <u>sensory neurone</u> to the CNS.

3) In the CNS the sensory neurone passes on the message to another type of neurone — a <u>relay neurone</u>.

4) The relay neurone <u>passes</u> the impulse to a <u>motor neurone</u>.

5) The impulse then travels along the motor neurone to the <u>effector</u> (in this example it's a muscle).

6) The <u>muscle</u> then <u>contracts</u> and moves your hand away from the bee.

7) An impulse always takes the <u>same</u>, <u>direct route</u> through the reflex arc so <u>no information</u> is ever <u>processed</u>. This is why reflexes are <u>involuntary</u> and <u>rapid</u>.

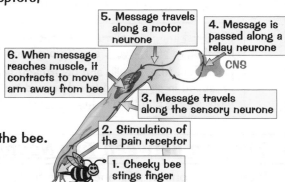

5. Message travels along a motor neurone

4. Message is passed along a relay neurone

CNS

6. When message reaches muscle, it contracts to move arm away from bee

3. Message travels along the sensory neurone

2. Stimulation of the pain receptor

1. Cheeky bee stings finger

Simple Reflexes Improve <u>the Chance of</u> Survival

<u>Simple animals</u>, such as jellyfish, have <u>no brain</u> — they rely <u>entirely</u> on <u>simple reflex</u> actions.
Simple reflexes cause these animals to <u>respond</u> to some stimuli in a way that <u>helps them survive</u>, for example:

<u>Finding food</u>: e.g. sea anemones wave their tentacles more when stimulated by chemicals emitted by their prey — this increases their chances of catching them.

<u>Sheltering from predators</u>: e.g. molluscs (things like mussels and clams) close their shells when they detect a predator — this decreases their chances of being eaten.

<u>Humans</u> also have <u>simple reflexes</u> that may <u>protect</u> them from damage or increase their chances of <u>survival</u>:

1) Very bright <u>light</u> can <u>damage</u> the <u>eye</u> — so there's a reflex to protect it. In very bright light muscles in the eye <u>contract</u> making the <u>pupil smaller</u>, allowing <u>less light</u> into the eye.

2) If a person picks up a <u>hot object</u> there's a reflex that makes them <u>drop</u> it.

3) <u>Newborn babies</u> have reflexes that are <u>lost</u> as they <u>develop</u>, for example:
   • they'll <u>automatically suckle</u> from their mothers.
   • they'll <u>grasp</u> when their palms are touched.
   • they'll try to <u>take steps</u> when their feet are put on a flat surface.

4) Your doctor might have tested your <u>knee jerk reflex</u> by tapping under your knee.

Don't get all twitchy — just learn it...

You <u>don't think about reflexes</u> — they just happen. Revision is not such an automatic process, unfortunately...

Modifying and Learning Reflexes

Reflexes are pretty handy, but it doesn't stop there — you can modify some of the reflexes you're born with if you need to and you can even learn new ones.

Reflex Responses can be Modified by the Brain

In some cases it's possible to modify a natural reflex response. Here's an example:

1) When you pick up a hot object such as a hot dinner plate you'll want to drop the plate — this is a reflex response to protect your skin from damage.

2) Dropping the plate might not be the best idea (you'd be left without any tea for one), but luckily reflex responses can be modified.

3) The response can be overridden by a neurone between the brain and the motor neurone of the reflex arc — the result is a little bit of pain but at least you've saved your dinner.

Reflex Responses can Also be Learned

A stimulus causes a particular reflex response, but animals can learn to produce the same response to a new (secondary) stimulus. This is called conditioning — the new reflex is called a conditioned reflex. The best example of this is Pavlov's dogs:

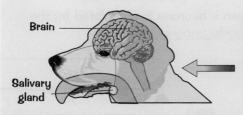

1) Pavlov studied the behaviour of dogs and noticed that they would salivate (drool) every time they smelt food.

2) This is a simple reflex in response to a primary stimulus (the smell of food).

3) He experimented by ringing a bell just before the dogs were given their food.

4) After a while he found that the dogs salivated when the bell was rung — even if they couldn't smell food.

5) The dogs responded to a secondary stimulus (the bell). This is a conditioned reflex. In a conditioned reflex, the final response (drooling) has no direct connection to the secondary stimulus.

Conditioned Reflexes can Increase Chances of Survival

Dogs drooling every time a bell rings doesn't really sound that useful — but that's not always the case. Some conditioned reflexes can increase an animal's chances of survival. Here's an example:

1) Instead of being camouflaged to match their surroundings, some insects are brightly coloured so that they stand out. This may sound a bit odd but there's a very good reason...

2) Insects with bright colouring are often poisonous — their bright colours act as a warning to predators (such as birds) that they'll probably taste pretty horrible and could even cause some harm.

3) The predators develop a conditioned reflex to the secondary stimulus (i.e. the colour of the insects).

4) For example, a bird spots a brightly coloured caterpillar. When the bird eats the caterpillar it notices that it doesn't taste too good and makes the bird feel ill. The bird associates the bad taste and illness with the colour and the next time it spots a caterpillar with that colouring, it avoids it.

5) By learning to avoid the poisonous insects, the birds are increasing their own chances of survival. Clever.

I condition my hair to make it lie down...

If this stuff pops up in the exam they might not necessarily give you the classic Pavlov example. You just have to apply what you know to the situation, identifying the simple and conditioned reflexes.

Brain Development and Learning

That great big spongy mass in your noggin helps you learn useful things like how to walk and talk, and not so useful things like how to play snap and do handstands. All animals with brains can learn things, but humans are much better at learning because we've evolved a much bigger brain. This has given us a survival advantage which explains why we're such a jolly successful species.

The Brain is Pretty Complex

The brain is basically a big bunch of neurones all interconnected — it contains billions of the things. This means that it can do clever things like:

* modify behaviour as a result of experience — i.e. learn stuff.
* coordinate complicated behaviour, e.g. social behaviour (interacting with other members of the group).

The Environment can Affect Brain Development and Learning

The brain develops at an early age

1) The brain of a newborn baby is only partly developed — most of the neurone connections are not yet formed. It becomes more and more developed with every new experience.

2) Connections form as the child experiences new things — when a neurone is stimulated by the experience it branches out, connecting cells that were previously unconnected.

3) By the age of about three most of the connections that will ever form have been formed — making a huge network of neurones with trillions of possible routes for nerve impulses to travel down. The number of connections remains constant until about age ten.

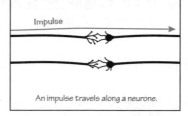

An impulse travels along a neurone.

The neurone responds by branching out.

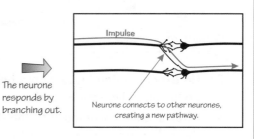

Neurone connects to other neurones, creating a new pathway.

You learn throughout your life

1) When experiences are repeated over and over again the pathways that the nerve impulses travel down become strengthened.

2) Strengthened pathways are more likely to transmit impulses than others.

3) This is why playing the piano is easier if you've practised a lot.

4) After the age of about ten the pathways that aren't used as often die off — that's why it's harder for older people to learn new things like a foreign language or how to use a computer (though new neurones and connections can still form in adults, which is why they can learn).

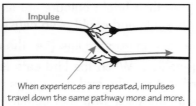

When experiences are repeated, impulses travel down the same pathway more and more.

This strengthens the connection

At around the age of ten the connections that are no longer used are deleted.

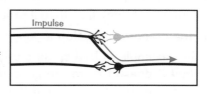

Strengthening pathways — usually done with tarmac...

This stuff is pretty complicated but you need to get your head round it. When you're really young you connect all your neurones, then the ones you use the most are strengthened and the others are pruned.

Learning Skills and Behaviour

Despite what you might think, <u>learning</u> is a <u>good thing</u> — without it you'd still be trying to figure out who that strange woman is that keeps making baby-faces at you...

Being Able to Learn Means You can Adapt to New Situations

1) Complex animals are incredibly <u>adaptable</u> — they're able to <u>cope</u> with whatever the <u>environment</u> throws at them.

2) They're adaptable because of the <u>variety</u> of <u>potential pathways</u> in the brain — there are <u>trillions</u>.

3) <u>Simpler animals</u> (like worms and insects) have <u>less flexible</u> nervous systems — they don't have anything like as many <u>pathways</u>, making their behaviour <u>more predictable</u> and much <u>less adaptable</u>.

Some Skills Only Develop at Certain Ages

Most scientists believe that there are definite <u>stages</u> in the <u>development</u> of a child's brain — some nerve pathways need to be strengthened at a <u>particular age</u>, otherwise it's <u>too late</u>. Here's an example:

1) The ability to <u>communicate</u> by <u>language</u> (talk) depends on a child <u>hearing other people speak</u>.

2) It is thought that they must hear this during a certain <u>critical period</u>. If children haven't learnt to talk by around the age of <u>ten</u> then they probably won't ever be able to.

3) Evidence to back this up comes from studies of <u>feral children</u> (children who have been raised by animals <u>without</u> any <u>human contact</u>, just like in the Jungle Book).

> A famous case was the <u>wild boy of Aveyron</u>, who was discovered around 200 years ago. He grew up in a <u>forest</u> in France. It's believed he was raised by <u>wolves</u>. He was about <u>12 years old</u> when he was discovered and although he showed signs of <u>intelligence</u>, he <u>never</u> learned to <u>speak</u>.

4) Similar children, discovered at a <u>younger age</u>, <u>have</u> been able to learn to talk. This evidence <u>supports</u> the idea of a critical period.

> One girl was discovered at the age of <u>eight</u>, <u>unable to speak</u>. After a short time with doctors she started to pick up <u>new words</u>. Although she never understood things like <u>grammar</u> she did develop a <u>vocabulary</u> of several hundred words.

The Cerebral Cortex is an Important Part of the Brain

The brain is a pretty <u>complex organ</u> — luckily the only part you need to know about is the <u>cerebral cortex</u>.

1) The cerebral cortex is the <u>outer part</u> of the brain.

2) It has a folded structure — this makes the brain look <u>wrinkled</u>.

3) The cerebral cortex plays a pretty big role in things like <u>intelligence</u>, <u>memory</u>, <u>language</u> and <u>consciousness</u>.

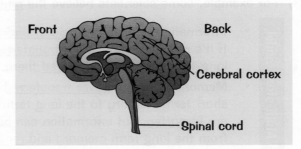

Front   Back

Cerebral cortex

Spinal cord

My sister looks like she was raised by wolves...

Okay so maybe it isn't "just like in the jungle book". When Mowgli meets the girl at the end, if he's missed the <u>critical period</u> chances are she isn't going to be too impressed by his <u>grunts</u>. Oh and don't get me started on the talking animals that dress up in grass skirts and dance just to befriend monkeys.

Studying the Brain

Scientists know a bit about the brain but not as much as they'd like to. Their knowledge is improving with the invention of new gadgetry that helps them study the brain. And as usual there are different theories...

Scientists Use a Range of Methods to Study the Brain

Scientists use a few different methods to study the brain and figure out which bits do what:

① **Studying patients with brain damage** — If a small part of the brain has been damaged the effect this has on the patient can tell you a lot about what the damaged part of the brain does. E.g. if an area at the back of the brain was damaged by a stroke and the patient went blind you know that that area has something to do with vision.

② **Electrically stimulating the brain** — The brain can be stimulated electrically by pushing a tiny electrode into the tissue and giving it a small zap of electricity. By observing what stimulating different parts of the brain does, it's possible to get an idea of what those parts do. E.g. when a certain part of the brain (know as the motor area) is stimulated, it causes muscle contraction and movement.

③ **MRI Scans** — A magnetic resonance imaging (MRI) scanner is a big fancy tube-like machine that can produce a very detailed picture of the brain's structures. Scientists use it to find out what areas of the brain are active when people are doing things like listening to music or trying to recall a memory.

Memory is the Storage and Retrieval of Information

To remember something first you have to store the information (i.e. learn it) and then you have to retrieve it. There are two main types of memory — short-term and long-term:

1) Short-term memory lasts for anything from a few seconds to a few hours. It's used for information that you're thinking about at the moment.

2) Long-term memories are memories that were stored days, months or even years ago.

Humans are more likely to remember things when they can see a pattern (or impose a pattern) in the information, e.g. remembering the phone number 123123 is a lot easier than remembering 638294. You're also more likely to remember things if the information is associated with strong stimuli, like bright lights and colours, strong smells or noises. It also helps if the information is repeated, especially if it's over a long time.

Memory Models Try to Explain How Memory Works

1) The problem with memory is that nobody knows for sure how it works.

2) There are loads of different models that try to explain it.

3) For example, some scientists believe the multi-store model offers a good explanation:

Multi-store model
- Information that you've paid attention to is temporarily stored in short-term memory. If it's repeated enough it's transferred to long-term memory and stored there.
- Memories that are never transferred from the short term memory to the long term memory are forgotten, but information can be retrieved from the long term memory and remembered.

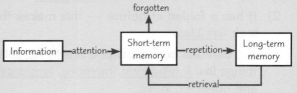

4) So far no model has provided a satisfactory explanation of human memory.

Memory's just like knitting — all you need is a good pattern...

Hopefully this should give you some handy revision tips. Repeating things helps lodge them in your long-term memory and using bright colours means you associate facts with a strong stimulus. Simple.

Revision Summary for Module B6

Hmm... so this whole nervous system and brain malarkey — I'll admit it's not the easiest topic in the world, but it's pretty interesting I reckon. And now you know why the only way to get stuff into your long-term memory for your exam is to repeat it over and over and over and over and over again... and on that note here's some questions to see whether any of the information you've just read has made it into your long-term storage space.

1) What is a stimulus?
2) Name the two organs that make up the CNS.
3) What do sensory neurones do?
4) Where do motor neurones carry signals to and from?
5) What are receptors? Give an example of a receptor.
6) What are effectors? Name two examples of an effector.
7) What is the role of the CNS?
8) Draw a diagram to show the pathway between a stimulus and a response.
9) How do neurones transmit information?
10) What is an axon?
11) What is the function of the fatty sheath surrounding some axons?
12) What is a synapse?
13) Describe how impulses are transmitted across a synapse.
14) Describe one way that the drug ecstasy can increase the concentration of serotonin in the brain.
15) What is a reflex?
16) Draw a diagram to show a reflex arc.
17) Give two ways that simple reflexes increase an animal's chance of survival.
18) Give three examples of simple reflexes in humans.
19) How are reflexes modified?
20) Give an example of when it would be advantageous to modify a reflex.
21) Briefly describe the experiment carried out by Pavlov on reflexes.
22) Describe another example of a conditioned reflex.
23) How can new experiences increase the number of connections in the brain of a child?
24) What happens to pathways when activities are repeated?
25) Why is it harder for older people to learn new things?
26) Why are complex animals better at adapting to new situations than simple animals?
27) Why is it important for children to develop their language skills at an early age?
Use an example of a feral child to explain your answer.
28) Name two things that the cerebral cortex of the brain is important for.
29) Give three methods used by scientists to study the brain.
30) What is memory?
31) Describe the model of multi-store memory.

Blood and The Circulatory System

Blood is really vital — it's that red stuff that travels through the circulatory system, carrying all the bits and bobs your cells need to stay alive. But it wouldn't get anywhere without the heart to pump it around.

Blood is a Fluid Made Up of Cells, Platelets and Plasma

1) Blood transports various substances around the body through the circulatory system. For example, blood carries oxygen and glucose to the muscles and takes carbon dioxide (a waste product), away from them.

2) Blood is made up of lots of different things:

RED BLOOD CELLS — The job of red blood cells is to transport oxygen from the lungs to the rest of the body. They don't have a nucleus so they can be packed full with haemoglobin — a substance that binds with oxygen. Red blood cells have a biconcave shape to give them a large surface area for exchanging oxygen.

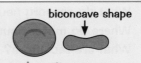
biconcave shape

PLASMA — This is the liquid that carries nutrients (e.g. glucose and amino acids), antibodies, hormones and waste (e.g. carbon dioxide and urea).

WHITE BLOOD CELLS — They help to fight infection by protecting your body against attack from microorganisms.

PLATELETS — These are small fragments of cells that help the blood to clot at the site of a wound.

Humans Have a Double Circulatory System

1) Humans have a double circulatory system — two circuits joined together.

2) The first one pumps deoxygenated blood (blood without oxygen) to the lungs to take in oxygen. The blood then returns to the heart.

3) The second one pumps oxygenated blood around the body. The blood gives up its oxygen at the body cells and the deoxygenated blood returns to the heart to be pumped out to the lungs again.

Lungs

Rest of Body

Learn This Diagram of the Heart with All Its Labels

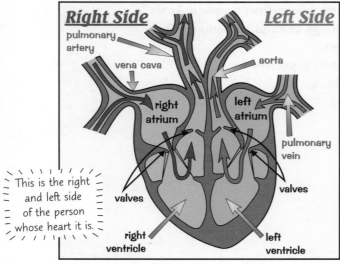

Right Side   **Left Side**
pulmonary artery
vena cava
aorta
right atrium
left atrium
pulmonary vein
valves
valves
This is the right and left side of the person whose heart it is.
right ventricle
left ventricle

1) The right atrium of the heart receives deoxygenated blood from the body (through the vena cava).

2) The deoxygenated blood moves through to the right ventricle, which pumps it to the lungs (via the pulmonary artery).

3) The left atrium receives oxygenated blood from the lungs (through the pulmonary vein).

4) The oxygenated blood then moves through to the left ventricle, which pumps it out round the whole body (via the aorta).

5) The valves in the heart prevent the backflow of blood — veins also have valves for this reason.

6) There are two coronary arteries which supply the heart muscle cells with blood.

7) The left ventricle wall is thicker than the right as it has to pump blood all the way around the body (the right only pumps to the lungs). The atria have thinner walls as they only pump blood to the ventricles.

The heart — it's all just pump and circumstance...

You need to know all of this stuff, so get learnin' — there's more on the marvellous circulatory system on page 22.

Tissue Fluid and The Skeletal System

Tissue fluid and bones — possibly the worst variety of soup in the world...

Chemicals are Exchanged Between Cells and Capillaries

Capillary Bed

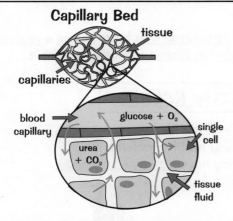

1) Arteries branch into capillaries, which are really tiny blood vessels.
2) They have permeable walls, so substances can diffuse in and out.
3) Networks of capillaries in tissue are called capillary beds.
4) As blood passes through capillary beds small molecules (e.g. water, glucose and oxygen) are forced out of the capillaries to form the tissue fluid, which surrounds the cells. These substances can then diffuse out of the tissue fluid into the cells.
5) Waste chemicals (e.g. carbon dioxide and urea) diffuse out of the cells into the tissue fluid, then into the capillaries.
6) The tissue fluid allows cells to get the substances they need and get rid of waste without a capillary supplying every single cell.

If You Didn't Have a Skeleton, You'd be Jelly-like

1) The job of a skeleton is to support the body and allow it to move — as well as protect vital organs.
2) Fish, amphibians, reptiles, birds and mammals are all vertebrates — they all have a backbone and an internal skeleton. Other animals (e.g. insects) have their skeleton on the outside.

Joints Allow the Bones to Move

1) The bones at a joint are held together by ligaments. Ligaments have a high tensile strength (i.e. you can pull them and they don't snap easily) but they are also slightly elastic (stretchy) — this means they help to stabilise joints but still allow movement.
2) The ends of bones are covered with a smooth layer of cartilage to reduce friction between the bones. Cartilage can be slightly compressed so it acts as a shock absorber, like a cushion between bones.
3) Membranes at some joints release oily synovial fluid to lubricate the joints, allowing them to move more easily by reducing friction.

Muscles Pull on Bones to Move Them

1) Bones are attached to muscles by tendons (which also attach muscles to other muscles).
2) Muscles move bones at a joint by contracting (becoming shorter).
3) Tendons can't stretch much so when a muscle contracts a tendon pulls on the bone, transmitting the force from the muscle to the bone.
4) Muscles can only pull on bones to move a joint — they can't push. This is why muscles usually come in pairs (called antagonistic pairs).
5) When one muscle in the pair contracts, the joint moves in one direction. When the other muscle contracts, it moves in the opposite direction.

The biceps and triceps are an antagonistic pair of muscles.

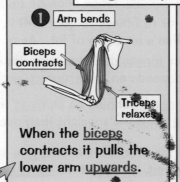
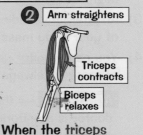

① Arm bends — Biceps contracts, Triceps relaxes. When the biceps contracts it pulls the lower arm upwards.

② Arm straightens — Triceps contracts, Biceps relaxes. When the triceps contracts the lower arm is pulled back down.

What's a skeleton's favourite instrument?... a trom-bone...

Bones are pretty sturdy, but if you wrench a joint you can dislocate it (see page 67) — and it's blummin' painful.

Exercise and Fitness

Exercise is pretty darn important for keeping you fit — and fitness can be measured...

Exercise **Helps to** Increase Fitness

1) Being fit is a measure of how well you can do physical activities.

2) Exercise increases fitness, and it's most effective when it's done in a structured way by following a regime. Fitness practitioners, like personal trainers and gym instructors, can design fitness regimes for people.

Information **is Needed to** Develop **the** Right Exercise Regime

Fitness practitioners need to have some essential background information, such as:

1) Health problems — the practitioner needs to know the symptoms of any health problems the person has that could affect their ability to exercise, for example if they have high blood pressure.

2) Current medication — some medications can affect a person's ability to exercise, e.g. by making them drowsy or affecting their coordination.

3) Previous fitness treatments — to know what has or hasn't worked before.

4) Other lifestyle factors — e.g. a person who smokes or drinks heavily should cut down on these so they can get the most benefit from the regime.

5) Family medical history — illnesses often run in families, so it could be important when designing a regime.

6) Physical activity — so the practitioner can plan a challenging programme that won't injure the client.

Heart Rate **and** Blood Pressure Increase **During** Exercise

1) When you're not exercising your heart rate and blood pressure are said to be at their resting levels.

2) During exercise your blood pressure and heart rate increase.

3) When you stop exercising your blood pressure and heart rate return to their resting levels. The time it takes for this to happen is called the recovery period.

4) The fitter you are, the shorter your recovery period.

Fitness **Can Be** Measured **in** Different Ways

1) Your body mass index (BMI) is based on your mass and height. It can be used as an indicator of your fitness:

$$BMI = \frac{body\ mass\ (kg)}{height^2\ (m^2)}$$

A fit person is likely to have a BMI in the 'normal' range.

Body Mass Index	Weight Description
below 18.5	underweight
18.5 – 24.9	normal
25 – 29.9	overweight
30 – 40	moderately obese
above 40	severely obese

2) BMI isn't always the most accurate indicator of fitness — for example, if you're fit and muscular your BMI might be outside the 'normal' range because muscle is more dense (heavier per unit of volume) than fat.

3) An alternative indicator of fitness to your BMI is your proportion of body fat — the percentage of your body mass that's made up of fat. As your fitness increases, your percentage lowers.

4) You can monitor your fitness during an exercise regime to see if you're improving. Any assessment of progress always depends on the accuracy and repeatability of the monitoring procedures:

ACCURACY — the results should be as close to what's actually happening as possible, e.g. if a doctor is monitoring someone's weight they need to be sure the scales they are using are accurate.

REPEATABILITY — the procedure should give reliable results. So, if the procedure was repeated, you'd get the same results (see page 77 for more).

My idea of an exercise regime — running to the pie shop every day...

You might get an exam question asking you to interpret data on this stuff — it'll be a lot easier if you've revised...

Exercise and Injury

Although exercise is <u>great</u> for your <u>fitness</u>, too much of it can cause <u>problems</u>...

Excessive Exercising *Can Cause* Injuries

Some <u>common injuries</u> that can result from <u>excessive exercise</u> are:

1) <u>Sprains</u> — damage to a <u>ligament</u> (see page 65), usually by being <u>stretched</u> too much. E.g. a twisted ankle is where the foot <u>turns over</u>, pulling the ligament <u>too far</u>, causing damage and <u>pain</u>.

2) <u>Dislocations</u> — a bone comes out of its <u>socket</u> (eek). For example, a heavy fall could cause a dislocation at the <u>shoulder</u>, causing <u>severe pain</u>. It also makes the joint look <u>weird</u> (because the bone is in the wrong position).

3) <u>Torn ligaments</u> — the ligament actually <u>tears</u>. This will cause more <u>severe pain</u> than a sprain and will often mean <u>loss of control</u> of the joint because the bones are no longer <u>attached</u> firmly together.

4) <u>Torn tendons</u> — a <u>tear</u> in the tendon that attaches the muscle to its bone. It occurs when a muscle <u>contracts</u> in one direction, but is being <u>pulled</u> in the opposite direction. And it's painful too.

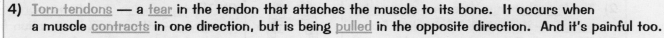

The <u>RICE</u> Method *Can be Used to* Treat Sprains

The main <u>symptoms</u> of a sprain are <u>pain</u> and <u>swelling</u> in the affected area. <u>Treatment</u> involves reducing these symptoms and creating the right conditions for the injury to <u>heal itself</u>. If a sprain is not too severe, it can be treated using the <u>RICE method</u>:

Rest — to <u>avoid</u> any further damage. This is especially important for the first <u>24</u> hours. Then, the joint can be slowly and <u>progressively</u> used more and more.

Ice — to help to <u>reduce swelling</u> (e.g. using a bag of frozen peas wrapped in a tea towel). It works by <u>reducing</u> the <u>temperature</u> and <u>blood flow</u> to the injured area.

Compression — a firm <u>bandage</u> is placed around the injured part to help <u>reduce swelling</u> and prevent further damage from <u>excessive</u> movement of the injured joint. You have to make sure it's <u>not too tight</u> or it'll <u>cut off the blood flow</u> to the area.

Elevation — <u>raising</u> an injured limb as high as possible to help <u>reduce swelling</u> by making it easier for blood to flow back to the heart.

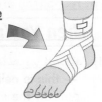

Physiotherapists *Treat* Skeletal-muscular Injuries

More <u>serious</u> injuries to the skeletal or muscular system will be treated by a <u>physiotherapist</u>. A physiotherapist may give <u>treatment</u> to reduce pain and swelling (e.g. RICE, cortisone injections) and <u>therapies</u> (e.g. laser treatment) to speed up healing. They will also <u>advise</u> on the <u>best exercises</u> to do to <u>rehabilitate</u> after an injury. These may be <u>graded exercises</u>, which steadily build up the <u>strength</u> of a muscle or joint. For example, for a <u>damaged knee</u>, the exercise might consist of —

1) Standing up and <u>tensing</u> the muscles <u>without</u> moving the knee.
2) Sitting with the lower leg hanging loose, then slowly <u>raising</u> and <u>lowering</u> the lower leg by bending the knee.
3) <u>Stepping</u> up and down, onto and off a <u>low box</u>.
4) Standing, and <u>bending</u> and <u>straightening</u> the legs at the knees.

Not guilty — the sporting verdict in juries...

Make sure you can <u>recall</u> every injury given here and know the <u>symptoms</u> of a <u>sprain</u> and how to <u>treat one</u>.

Controlling Body Temperature

The body has to keep its insides at around <u>37 °C</u> — the <u>optimum temperature</u> for lots of important <u>reactions</u>.

Body Temperature **Must be Kept** Constant

1) The body has to <u>balance</u> the amount of <u>heat energy gained</u> (e.g. through respiration) and <u>lost</u> to keep the <u>core body temperature constant</u>.

2) <u>Temperature receptors</u> in the <u>skin</u> detect the <u>external temperature</u>, and receptors in the <u>hypothalamus</u> (a part of the <u>brain</u>) detect the temperature of the <u>blood</u>.

3) The <u>nervous system</u> (see page 56) helps to control body temperature, using the following <u>negative feedback</u> mechanism (see page 25)...

> Core body temperature is the temperature inside your body, where your organs are.

1) <u>Temperature receptors</u> detect that core body temperature is <u>too high</u>.

2) The <u>hypothalamus</u> acts as a <u>processing centre</u> — it receives information from the temperature receptors and <u>triggers</u> the <u>effectors</u> automatically.

3) <u>Effectors</u>, e.g. sweat glands, produce a <u>response</u> (see below) and <u>counteract</u> the change.

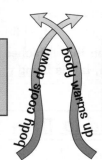
body cools down / *body warms up*

1) <u>Temperature receptors</u> detect that core body temperature is <u>too low</u>.

2) The <u>hypothalamus</u> acts as a <u>processing centre</u> — it receives information from the temperature receptors and <u>triggers</u> the <u>effectors</u> automatically.

3) <u>Effectors</u>, e.g. muscles, produce a <u>response</u> (see below) and <u>counteract</u> the change.

Some effectors work <u>antagonistically</u>, e.g. one effector heats and another cools — they'll work at the same time to achieve a very precise temperature. This mechanism allows a <u>more sensitive response</u>.

The Body has Some Nifty Tricks for Altering its Temperature

<u>Different responses</u> are produced by <u>effectors</u> to <u>counteract</u> an increase or decrease in <u>body temperature</u>.

When You're TOO HOT:

1) <u>Blood vessels</u> close to the skin's surface get <u>bigger in diameter</u> — this is called <u>vasodilation</u>. This means that <u>more blood</u> gets to the <u>surface</u> of the skin. The warm blood then <u>loses more of its heat</u> to the surroundings.

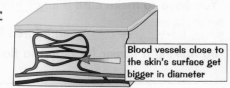
Blood vessels close to the skin's surface get bigger in diameter

2) Your sweat glands produce <u>more sweat</u> — when the water in the sweat <u>evaporates</u> heat is used, which <u>cools</u> the body. If you sweat a lot, e.g. when <u>exercising</u>, the <u>water loss</u> may cause you to become <u>dehydrated</u>. If you're dehydrated you'll produce far <u>less sweat</u>, which means your core body <u>temperature</u> will <u>increase</u>.

When You're TOO COLD:

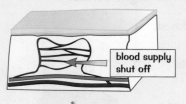
blood supply shut off

1) <u>Blood vessels</u> close to the skin's surface get <u>smaller in diameter</u> — this is called <u>vasoconstriction</u>. This means that <u>less blood</u> gets to the <u>surface</u> of the skin, which <u>stops</u> the blood losing as much heat to the surroundings.

2) You <u>shiver</u> — your <u>muscles contract rapidly</u>. This <u>increases</u> the rate of <u>respiration</u> and warms the tissue surrounding the muscles.

Sweaty and red — I'm so attractive in the heat...

So, your <u>body</u> is pretty good at <u>regulating</u> its <u>temperature</u> in everyday situations. Make sure you know there are <u>temperature receptors</u> in the <u>skin</u> and <u>hypothalamus</u> and learn <u>how</u> the body deals with changes in temperature.

Controlling Blood Sugar

Your body has to control the <u>level</u> of <u>sugar</u> in the blood, and it does this using a <u>hormone</u> called <u>insulin</u>. However, if a person suffers from <u>diabetes</u> their body <u>can't</u> control their blood sugar level properly.

Insulin <u>Controls</u> Blood Sugar <u>Level</u>

1) <u>Eating foods</u> that are <u>high</u> in <u>simple sugars</u>, e.g. <u>processed foods</u> like cereals and biscuits, causes your <u>blood sugar level</u> to <u>rise rapidly</u>.

2) This is because simple sugars are <u>digested</u> and <u>absorbed</u> into your blood really <u>quickly</u>.

3) The <u>level</u> of <u>sugar</u> in your <u>blood</u> needs to be kept <u>steady</u> — your body uses <u>insulin</u> to control it.

4) When the blood sugar level gets <u>too high</u>, the pancreas <u>releases insulin</u> which causes <u>sugar</u> to be <u>removed</u> from the <u>blood</u>.

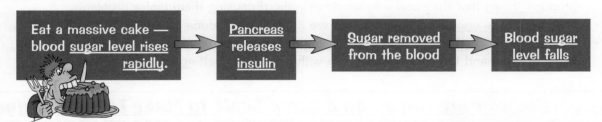

Diabetes <u>is Where</u> Blood Sugar <u>Level</u> Can't <u>be Controlled</u> Properly

There are <u>two</u> types of diabetes:

Type 1 <u>Diabetes</u>

1) <u>Type 1</u> diabetes is where the <u>pancreas stops producing insulin</u>.

2) This means that the <u>blood sugar</u> level of a person suffering from type 1 diabetes can <u>rise</u> to a <u>dangerous level</u>.

3) It's <u>controlled</u> by <u>insulin therapy</u> — this usually involves injecting insulin into the blood, often <u>at mealtimes</u>. The injection has to have the <u>right amount</u> of insulin to make sure the body <u>doesn't remove too much</u> sugar.

Type 2 <u>Diabetes</u>

1) <u>Type 2</u> diabetes is sometimes called <u>late onset diabetes</u> as it usually develops <u>later in life</u>. Having a <u>poor diet</u> or being <u>obese</u> increases the <u>risk</u> of developing this type of diabetes.

2) This type of diabetes occurs when the <u>body no longer responds</u> to its <u>own insulin</u>, or it <u>doesn't make enough</u> insulin. This can cause a person's <u>blood sugar</u> level to <u>rise</u> to a <u>dangerous level</u>.

3) It can be <u>controlled</u> by <u>exercising</u> and eating a carefully <u>controlled diet</u>:

> For example, someone who suffers from <u>type 2</u> diabetes can <u>keep</u> their blood sugar at a <u>steady level</u> by eating foods that are <u>high</u> in <u>fibre</u> and <u>complex carbohydrates</u>. These foods are <u>digested more slowly</u> than simple sugars, so the sugar is <u>absorbed</u> into the blood over a <u>longer period</u> of time. This means that the <u>blood sugar</u> level <u>rises more slowly</u> and the body can <u>remove</u> the sugar (e.g. by using it for respiration) <u>before</u> it becomes <u>too high</u>.

Sugars are carbohydrates.

<u>And people used to think the pancreas was just a cushion...</u> (true)

Examiners love writing questions where you have to <u>interpret data</u> so don't be surprised if they throw you one on how a poor diet can cause things like <u>diabetes</u>, some <u>cancers</u> and <u>heart disease</u>. They tend to look horrible but the trick is not to panic. Make sure you <u>read</u> through the data <u>carefully</u> and understand what they're asking.

The Industrial Use of Microorganisms

Microorganisms might not seem very special, but some of them are used in different industries to make things like medicines and food on a large scale. I think those microorganisms need a little more r-e-s-p-e-c-t...

Some Features of Microorganisms Make Them Ideal for Industrial Use

Microorganisms (like bacteria and fungi) are pretty darn useful for making products on an industrial scale. Here are a few reasons why:

- They reproduce rapidly under the right conditions, so products can be made quickly.
- They have plasmids — these can be genetically modified (see page 71) so you can make the microorganism produce the product you need.
- Their biochemistry is quite simple — fewer reactions happen in microorganisms than in humans, for example. This means you can make the microorganism produce things that they normally wouldn't without causing them major problems.
- They can make complex molecules that are difficult to produce artificially.
- There aren't any ethical concerns with using microorganisms — you could grow loads of them and throw them in the bin without anyone batting an eyelid (aww...).

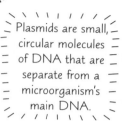

Plasmids are small, circular molecules of DNA that are separate from a microorganism's main DNA.

Microorganisms are Grown on a Large Scale to Make Lots of Products

Large amounts of microorganisms are grown in containers called fermenters. The conditions inside fermenters are kept at the optimum for growth to get the biggest possible amount of desirable products — you need to know about a few of these products:

ANTIBIOTICS — Some types of bacteria and fungi can be used to produce medicines on a large scale. E.g. penicillin is an antibiotic made by growing *Penicillium* mould (a type of fungus) in a fermenter.

FOOD FROM FUNGI — A type of single-celled protein made by fungi is used to make meat substitutes for vegetarian meals, e.g. Quorn™.

ENZYMES FOR MAKING FOOD — Enzymes are needed to make some types of food, e.g. cheese.
1) Traditionally cheese is made using a mix of enzymes called rennet from the lining of a calf's stomach.
2) Now chymosin (the important enzyme in rennet) can be produced by genetically modified microorganisms (see page 71) in large quantities — it's used as a vegetarian substitute for rennet.

ENZYMES FOR WASHING POWDER — Enzymes produced by bacteria can be used to make biological washing powders because they help to break down stains. For example, amylase enzymes can remove carbohydrate stains (e.g. jam and chocolate) and lipases can get rid of fat stains (e.g. butter and oil).

BIOFUELS — microorganisms can be used to make fuel, for example:
1) Yeast can be used to produce ethanol, a waste product of anaerobic respiration (see page 43). In some countries, e.g. Brazil, cars are adapted to run on a mixture of ethanol and petrol — this is known as 'gasohol'.
2) Microorganisms can be used to produce biogas — a fuel that's used for things like heating, cooking and lighting. It's made by the fermentation of plant and animal waste containing carbohydrates (see page 43).

My name's Andy and I'm addicted to biofuels. GASOHOLICS ANONYMOUS

So this isn't the petrol support group...?

My brother makes food from microorganisms — he's a fungi...

Bacteria and fungi aren't always the bad guys. They help us to produce delicious veggie meals, antibiotics, useful enzymes and fuel — it's not all disease and mould. Maybe they just need better PR.

Genetic Modification

Genetic modification — playing around with genes. Cool.

Genes can be Transferred Between Organisms

1) You need to know what <u>genetic modification</u> is:

> GENETIC MODIFICATION is where a GENE from one ORGANISM is TRANSFERRED to ANOTHER.

2) The <u>organism</u> with the <u>transferred gene</u> will then <u>produce</u> a <u>protein</u> using instructions in that gene.

3) The protein can be made <u>even though</u> the gene came from <u>another organism</u> because <u>all organisms</u> use the <u>same genetic code</u> (see page 49).

Genetic Modification Involves These Important Stages:

1) First the <u>gene</u> that's responsible for producing the <u>desirable protein</u> is <u>isolated</u> — its <u>position</u> on the source DNA is <u>identified</u>.

2) The useful gene is then <u>replicated</u> to create <u>lots</u> of <u>copies</u>.

3) Each gene is <u>joined</u> to a <u>vector</u> — a <u>carrier</u> for the gene which makes it <u>easier</u> to insert into a new cell. <u>Plasmids</u> and <u>viruses</u> are often used as vectors.

4) Vectors containing the useful gene are <u>transferred</u> into <u>new cells</u>, e.g. bacterial cells.

5) <u>Not all</u> of the new cells will be <u>modified</u>, e.g. the vector might not have been transferred properly.

6) So, the last stage is to <u>select</u> (identify) the individuals that have been <u>successfully modified</u>.

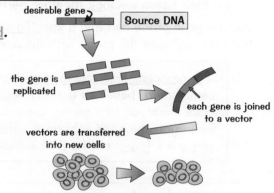

desirable gene → Source DNA

the gene is replicated

each gene is joined to a vector

vectors are transferred into new cells

the individual cells that have been successfully modified are selected

Genetic Modification has Useful Applications for Humans

There are a <u>couple of applications</u> of genetic modification that you need to know about:

MAKING MEDICINES

Genetically modified <u>bacteria</u> have been used to make <u>medicines</u> <u>cheaply</u>, <u>quickly</u> and in <u>large quantities</u>. For example:

1) <u>Insulin</u> is a <u>hormone</u> that's used to treat Type 1 <u>diabetes</u> (see page 69).

2) The gene for <u>human insulin production</u> can be <u>transferred</u> into <u>bacteria</u>.

3) The bacteria are grown in a <u>fermenter</u>, and the human insulin is simply <u>extracted</u> as it's produced.

4) This means that the insulin made by the bacteria is <u>exactly</u> the <u>same</u> as <u>human insulin</u>, so there's <u>less chance</u> of patients having an <u>allergic reaction</u> to it.

MAKING CROPS HERBICIDE-RESISTANT

1) Some plants have <u>natural resistance</u> to things like <u>herbicides</u> (weedkillers).

2) Thanks to genetic modification we can <u>cut out</u> the gene responsible and stick it into <u>any useful plant we like</u>, e.g. potato plants.

3) <u>Herbicide-resistant crops</u> are <u>useful</u> to farmers because they can use a <u>really effective</u> weedkiller <u>without damaging</u> their <u>produce</u>.

4) However, <u>herbicide-resistant crops</u> can be <u>more expensive</u> than <u>normal crops</u>. Some people are worried that the <u>gene</u> might be <u>transferred</u> into <u>wild plants</u> (e.g. weeds), making them <u>hard</u> to <u>kill</u>.

5) Herbicide-resistant crops could <u>encourage</u> the use of <u>weedkillers</u>. This could <u>reduce biodiversity</u>, and it's possible the weed killers could <u>pollute water systems</u> or get into <u>food chains</u>.

It's another bloomin' herbicide.

Looks like poor Basil didn't even try to resist.

POLICE LINE: DO NOT CROSS

If only there was a gene to make revision easier...

You can do great things with genetic modification. But some people worry that we <u>don't know enough</u> about it, or that some <u>maniac</u> is going to come along and combine the Prime Minister with a grapefruit. Possibly.

Biological Technologies

There are lots of dead exciting (no, really) biological technologies — you need to know about four of them...

Genetic Testing **Can Help** Identify Genetic Disorders

You've already come across genetic testing (see page 13) — now you need to know how you could test for a genetic disorder that's caused by a faulty gene:

1) **TAKE A DNA SAMPLE** — DNA isolated from white blood cells is often used to test for genetic disorders — it's quick and easy to take a blood sample, which contains loads of white blood cells.

2) **MAKE A GENE PROBE** — to identify a faulty gene you can produce a gene probe. This is a strand of bases that's complementary to the faulty gene that you're looking for.

3) **USE THE GENE PROBE** — the gene probe is mixed with the DNA. If the gene is present the probe will stick to it — their bases will lock together perfectly. Just like this...

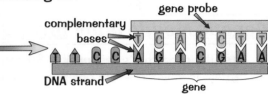

So, the gene probe can find a specific sequence of bases. But you can't see the probe with the naked eye...

A fluorescent chemical marker is stuck on the end of the sequence of bases so you can locate the gene probe once it's stuck to a gene. The marker will fluoresce (glow) when you shine UV light on it. The marker shows if the faulty gene is present, and where it's found on the DNA sample — the chromosome it's on might look a bit like this...

Nanotechnology **can** Improve Packaging Properties

Nanotechnology is a new technology that uses tiny structures that are about the size of some molecules.

1) Food can be made to last longer, e.g. adding clay nanoparticles to plastic makes the packaging better at keeping out oxygen and moisture. Some nanoparticles can kill harmful microorganisms.

2) Some 'smart packaging' uses nanoparticles to change the packaging's properties depending on the conditions. E.g. a milk carton could be made to change colour when the milk goes off.

Stem Cell Technology **Can be** Used **to** Treat Illnesses

Tissues and organs grown from stem cells can be used to treat illnesses. For example:

1) Leukaemia is a cancer of the blood or bone marrow. It's been successfully treated using stem cell technology. Bone marrow transplants can be used to replace the faulty bone marrow in patients suffering from leukaemia. Bone marrow contains stem cells that can become specialised to form any type of blood cell. The stem cells in the transplanted bone marrow produce healthy blood cells.

Take a look back at your Modules B1 and B5 notes for more on stem cells.

2) In the future, stem cells could be used to treat spinal cord injuries by replacing damaged nerve tissue.

Biomedical Engineering **Can Create** Replacement Body Parts

Biomedical engineering uses engineering technologies to improve human health — this includes creating replacement body parts. For example:

1) The heart has a group of cells which determine how fast it beats. If they stop working the heartbeat becomes irregular, which can be dangerous. The cells can be replaced with an artificial device called a pacemaker. It's implanted under the skin and it produces an electric current to control the heartbeat.

2) Faulty heart valves can also be replaced — either with animal or mechanical valves.

Nanatechnology — stair lifts, zimmer frames and slippers...

Thrilling fact of the day — learning about these four technologies could pick you up marks in the exam. Hurrah.

Ecosystems

Before we get any further into ecosystems you need to know a bit about <u>perfect closed loop systems</u> first...

All Outputs **are** Recycled **Within** Perfect Closed Loop Systems

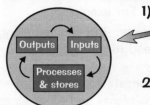

A <u>perfect closed loop</u> system

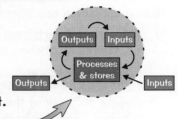

1) In a <u>perfect closed loop</u> system, <u>all</u> the <u>outputs</u> from processes or stores within the system are <u>recycled</u> — they're used as <u>inputs</u> to other processes or stores in the system.

2) There are <u>no outputs</u> from a <u>perfect closed loop</u> system (there's <u>no waste</u>) and there are <u>no inputs</u> to it.

3) However, most systems <u>aren't</u> perfect closed loops — they have <u>inputs</u> to them and <u>outputs</u> from them too.

Ecosystems **are a Type of** Closed Loop System

<u>Ecosystems</u> are a type of <u>closed loop system</u> because <u>most</u> of the <u>waste</u> (<u>output</u>) produced by organisms <u>isn't lost</u> — it's <u>recycled</u> as <u>food</u> or <u>reactants</u> for other organisms in the system. For example:

An ecosystem is all the living organisms in an area plus all the non-living stuff like soil, air and water.

1) <u>Oxygen</u> is a <u>waste product</u> produced by plants during <u>photosynthesis</u>. It's used by plants, animals and microorganisms as a <u>reactant</u> during <u>respiration</u>.

2) <u>Carbon dioxide</u> is a <u>waste product</u> produced during <u>respiration</u>. It's used by plants as a <u>reactant</u> during <u>photosynthesis</u>.

3) <u>Dead organic matter</u> (e.g. fallen petals, leaves, fruits and faeces) is used by <u>microorganisms</u> as <u>food</u>.

4) <u>Mineral nutrients</u> (e.g. nitrogen) are produced by <u>microorganisms</u> when their <u>digestive enzymes</u> break down organic matter. These nutrients are <u>absorbed</u> and <u>used</u> by plants.

My babies!

5) Many organisms like fish and plants, produce <u>large quantities</u> of <u>reproductive structures</u> (e.g. eggs, sperm, pollen, flowers and fruits). They have to do this because <u>most</u> of the structures <u>won't</u> grow into <u>adult organisms</u>. The ones that don't become adult organisms are <u>recycled</u> in the ecosystem (they're <u>eaten</u> by other organisms).

Stable Ecosystems **have** Balanced Inputs **and** Outputs

1) <u>No ecosystem</u> is a <u>perfect closed loop system</u> because <u>some</u> outputs are <u>always lost</u>. For example:
   - Some dead <u>organic matter</u> and <u>nutrients</u> can be <u>carried out</u> of an ecosystem by <u>air</u> or <u>water</u> — e.g. fallen leaves may be blown away by winds or carried away by rivers.
   - Some organisms <u>migrate</u> (move) from one ecosystem to another.

2) In a <u>stable ecosystem</u>, e.g. a rainforest, theses <u>outputs</u> (losses) are balanced by <u>gains</u>. For example, <u>a lot</u> of <u>water</u> is <u>lost</u> from a <u>rainforest</u> ecosystem as it flows out through <u>rivers</u>, but this output is <u>balanced</u> by the <u>gain</u> of water from the <u>high level</u> of <u>rainfall</u> in the ecosystem.

3) <u>Large amounts</u> of <u>vegetation</u> grow in <u>stable ecosystems</u> like <u>rainforests</u>. Vegetation is <u>beneficial</u> to ecosystems in a number of ways, for example:

   - It <u>reduces soil erosion</u> (where <u>soil</u> is <u>lost</u> from an ecosystem, e.g. by being <u>washed</u> or <u>blown away</u>). For example, <u>leaves</u> help to <u>protect soil</u> from <u>direct rainfall</u> (which can break up soil) and <u>roots</u> help to <u>bind</u> the soil together.
   - It <u>prevents extremes of temperatures</u>.
   - It <u>promotes cloud formation</u>.

Spaghetti hoops — a tastier kind of closed loop...

In your exam you might get asked to <u>interpret data</u> on the <u>storage</u> or <u>movement</u> of chemicals (like <u>water</u>, <u>carbon</u>, <u>oxygen</u> and <u>nitrogen</u>) in an ecosystem — but don't worry, <u>learning this page</u> should make it easier to understand.

Human Impacts On Ecosystems

Without ecosystems we'd be pretty stuffed — but a lot of the things we do can damage them...

Humans Activities Can Damage Ecosystems

Human activities can unbalance natural ecosystems by changing inputs and outputs. For example:

1) Farmers use fertilisers to give plants extra nutrients, e.g. nitrates, to help them grow. But this unbalances ecosystems because the input of nutrients is much higher than normal. It can lead to eutrophication:

> Nitrates from fertilised fields can be washed into rivers and lakes by rain. The nitrates cause lots of algae to grow at the surface of the water which prevents light from reaching the plants and other algae below. Eventually these organisms die because they can't photosynthesise. Bacteria decompose the dead material and use up oxygen. This oxygen isn't replaced because photosynthesis is only taking place at the surface. Animals that need oxygen from the water lower down (e.g. fish) will suffocate.

2) Humans take biomass out of ecosystems for their own use — this can damage an ecosystem:
   - Over-fishing removes a food source for some of the organisms in a food chain.
   - Unsustainable timber harvesting removes habitats and food sources for some organisms.

   There's more about sustainability on the next page.

3) Humans often clear natural areas of vegetation in ecosystems so they can grow agricultural crops and raise livestock. These activities can cause major problems:
   - They can reduce the biodiversity of an ecosystem (see page 32).
   - They can increase soil erosion. Increased soil erosion can lead to the silting of rivers, where soil is washed into rivers — making them more likely to flood because they can hold less water. It can also cause desertification — where land becomes infertile, so it can't support a lot of vegetation.

4) Human activities create non-recyclable waste, e.g. heavy metals (like mercury), that can't be used again within a system. This waste can build up to harmful levels in an ecosystem:

> For example, if heavy metal waste is released into water it can be eaten by small organisms and stored in their tissues in small amounts. Lots of those small organisms will be eaten by a predator — so a much larger amount of the heavy metal will be stored in the predator's tissues, which may be enough to kill it. As you go up the food chain the amount of waste in an organism will increase (or accumulate) — this process is called bioaccumulation.

Human Systems Aren't Closed Loop Systems

Human systems (systems that involve humans in some way) for example, those found in households, agriculture and industry, aren't closed loop systems. Here are a couple of reasons why:

1) Human systems create non-recyclable waste (waste that can't be used again in a system, see above).

2) Many human systems use fossil fuels, such as crude oil, as an energy source.
   There are a few reasons why using fossil fuels means that human systems aren't closed loops:

   - Using fossil fuels produces waste emissions (gases) that aren't used again in the system.
   - When fossil fuels are used it inputs energy into the system from outside the system. The energy in the fossil fuels came from the Sun, millions of years ago (fossil sunlight energy).
   - Fossil fuels take millions of years to form from the decay of dead organisms, but only seconds to use. Because they take so long to form, they can't be made again within the system.

The other fossils fuels won't talk to oil anymore — it was being crude...

Lots of the things we do can damage ecosystems — but on the next page you'll find ways to protect them...

Managing Ecosystems

We rely on ecosystems for loads of stuff, so we need to protect them. Luckily there are a few ways of doing this, and they revolve around the wonderful concept of sustainability...

Humans Rely on Ecosystems

1) Ecosystems provide us with clean air, water and food, e.g. fish and game (animals like pheasants).

2) Ecosystems also provide humans with fertile soil that's full of mineral nutrients — this is needed to produce crops.

3) Most crop production also needs pollination (the transfer of pollen grains between plants so they can be fertilised). Pollination is a sort of 'ecosystem service' that's carried out by organisms (e.g. bees) and things like the wind.

Humans Need to Use Resources in a Sustainable Way

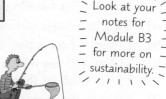

Look at your notes for Module B3 for more on sustainability.

1) Sustainability means meeting the needs of today's population without harming the environment so that future generations can still meet their own needs.

2) One part of this is using natural resources at a rate at which they can be replaced naturally. Here are a couple of ways that it can be done:

> 1) Fishing quotas (a quota is a fixed amount of something) have been introduced to prevent some types of fish, such as cod, from becoming extinct in certain areas through over-fishing. This means they'll still be around in years to come.
>
> 2) To make the production of wood and paper sustainable there are laws in some places insisting that logging companies plant new trees to replace those that they've cut down.

Sunlight is a Sustainable Source of Energy

1) The Sun's energy is sustainable because it can't be used up by human activities — the amount of sunlight that reaches the Earth in the future will not be affected by how much sunlight we use in the present.

2) Sunlight is used as a sustainable energy source in natural ecosystems to make food by photosynthesis (see page 44). The sunlight energy is initially stored in the form of carbohydrates and the energy is transferred between organisms when they're eaten.

3) Sunlight can also be a sustainable source of energy for sustainable agriculture:

- Sustainable agriculture aims to meet the food needs of today's population without preventing future generations from meeting their own needs, e.g. by not using up resources or damaging ecosystems.

- Sunlight could be used to power equipment used in sustainable agriculture, for example heating and lighting systems in greenhouses and irrigation systems.

Conserving Natural Ecosystems May Conflict With Community Needs

1) Sometimes communities have to decide between causing damage to an ecosystem to get the resources they need, and protecting an ecosystem but getting fewer resources from it.

2) For example, population growth in many areas means that more people have to be fed.

3) This causes tensions — people have to decide if it's worth increasing food production, e.g. by fishing more or producing more crops, at the risk of damaging an ecosystem, e.g. by removing organisms faster than they can be replaced or by increasing desertification (see page 74).

You are my sunshine, my only sunshine, you make me sustainable energy...

There's no getting around it — we need to protect our ecosystems. Just think, without ecosystems we wouldn't have fish for fish and chips or paper for loo rolls. Mind you, we wouldn't have oxygen, either...

Revision Summary for Module B7

This module is a mixed bag of biology fun — it's got everything. There's a bit of physiology, a dash of exercise, and a great helping of genetics... not to mention those lovely biological technologies and ecosystems. It's really important that you learn it all. See how well you're doing by trying to answer this terrific selection of questions.

1) a) Name three components of blood.
   b) Describe the function of each of these components.
2) Give two features of red blood cells which makes them ideal for transporting oxygen around the body.
3) What is meant by a double circulatory system?
4) Name the arteries that carry blood to a) the lungs and b) the body.
5) What do valves in the heart and veins do?
6) Describe how tissue fluid is formed.
7) What is the function of tissue fluid?
8) Give two ways of reducing friction in joints.
9) Describe how a pair of muscles moves a bone up and down.
10) a) Name three things a fitness practitioner needs to know when developing an exercise regime.
    b) For each of these, explain why the fitness practitioner needs to know about them.
11) What is the recovery period?
12) Give two ways of measuring fitness.
13) Other than a sprain, give two common injuries resulting from excessive exercise.
14) Describe how to treat a sprain.
15) Name the area of the brain that detects the temperature of the blood.
16) Describe your body's responses when its temperature increases.
17) Describe the function of insulin.
18) What is the difference between type 1 and type 2 diabetes?
19) a) Describe how to control type 1 diabetes.
    b) Describe how type 2 diabetes can be controlled.
20) Give five features of microorganisms that make them ideal for use in biotechnology.
21) Name one medicine that's produced on a large scale by microorganisms.
22) Describe two ways that microorganisms are involved in the production of food.
23) What is genetic modification?
24) Outline the stages involved in the genetic modification of a bacterial cell.
25) Give two examples of applications of genetic modification.
26) Outline the stages involved in genetic testing.
27) Give two uses of nanotechnology in the food industry.
28) Describe how stem cell technology has been used to treat leukaemia.
29) What is a perfect closed loop system?
30) a) Give three examples of waste products in natural ecosystems.
    b) How are they used by other organisms in ecosystems?
31) a) Why do some organisms produce loads of reproductive structures?
    b) Explain why this strategy isn't wasteful in stable ecosystems.
32) Describe the process of eutrophication.
33) What is bioaccumulation?
34) Describe one other way that humans unbalance ecosystems.
35) Name three things that humans need ecosystems for.
36) Suggest two ways that humans can use the resources in an ecosystem sustainably.
37) Suggest a reason why humans might choose not to protect an ecosystem.

Planning

Your controlled assessment is a <u>practical investigation</u>. To start with, you'll be given some material to get your head around. Here's what you'll need to do:

1) Come up with a <u>hypothesis</u>, then make a <u>prediction</u> based on your hypothesis that you can <u>test</u>.

2) <u>Plan</u> an experiment to test your prediction. You'll need to think about things like:

   - What you're going to <u>measure</u> and <u>how</u> you're going to do it (your <u>method</u>).
   - What <u>equipment</u> you're going to use (and <u>why</u> that equipment is <u>right for the job</u>).
   - How you're going to make sure your results are <u>accurate</u> and <u>reliable</u>.
   - The <u>range of values</u> and the <u>interval</u> (gap) between the values of the <u>independent variable</u>.

3) Write a <u>risk assessment</u> for the experiment.

4) <u>Explain</u> all the choices you made when planning the experiment.

Here are a few <u>tips</u> to help you with the planning stage:

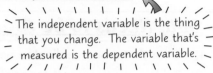

The independent variable is the thing that you change. The variable that's measured is the dependent variable.

Think Carefully About the Method and Equipment You'll Use

1) You should <u>test</u> several <u>different methods</u> before you start — this will help you decide which is the <u>best one</u> to use. You'll need to be able to <u>justify your choice</u> of method when writing up your experiment.

2) You need to make sure your method produces <u>reliable results</u>, i.e. results that can be <u>consistently reproduced</u> each time you do an experiment. If your results are reliable they're more likely to be <u>true</u>.

3) Your results will end up being more <u>reliable</u> if you make sure your method is a <u>fair test</u>:

   - In a lab experiment you usually <u>change one variable</u> and <u>measure</u> how it affects the <u>other variable</u>.

     > EXAMPLE: you might change only the temperature of an enzyme-controlled reaction and measure how it affects the rate of reaction.

   - To make it a fair test <u>everything else</u> that could affect the results should <u>stay the same</u> (otherwise you can't tell if the thing that's being changed is causing the results or not).

     > EXAMPLE continued: you need to keep the pH the same, otherwise you won't know if any change in the rate of reaction is caused by the change in temperature, or the change in pH.

4) <u>Repeating</u> the readings and calculating the <u>mean</u> (average) will also help your results to be more reliable.

5) You should also make sure that your results are <u>accurate</u>. This means that they're <u>really close</u> to the <u>true answer</u>. There are things you can do to make your results more accurate, such as using equipment that's <u>sensitive enough</u> to accurately measure the chemicals you're using. E.g. if you need to measure out 11 ml of a liquid, you'll need to use a measuring cylinder that can measure to 1 ml, not 5 or 10 ml.

Trial Runs Help Figure out the Range and Interval of Variable Values

1) A <u>trial run</u> is a <u>quick version</u> of your experiment.

2) Trial runs are used to figure out the <u>range</u> of variable values used (the upper and lower limit).

3) And they're used to figure out the <u>interval</u> (gap) between the values too.

> EXAMPLE continued:
> You might do trial runs at 10, 20, 30, 40 and 50 °C. If there was no reaction at 10 or 50 °C, you might narrow the range to 20-40 °C.
>
> If using 10 °C intervals gives you a big change in rate of reaction you might decide to use 5 °C intervals, e.g. 20, 25, 30, 35, 40 °C.

Experiments Must be Safe

1) Part of planning an investigation is making sure that it'll be <u>safe</u>.

2) You should always make sure that you <u>identify</u> all the hazards that you might encounter.

3) You should also come up with ways of <u>reducing the risks</u> from the hazards you've identified.

4) Do this by carrying out a <u>risk assessment</u>. E.g. if you're using a <u>Bunsen burner</u>, there would be a <u>fire risk</u> — you'd need to take <u>precautions</u> such as keeping flammable chemicals away from the flame.

Processing the Data

Once you've planned your experiment you'll carry it out to <u>collect your own data</u> (called <u>primary data</u>). You'll then be <u>given</u> some <u>secondary data</u> (that's data <u>collected by someone else</u>). You'll also need to <u>collect more secondary data</u> yourself, e.g. from textbooks, websites or even from <u>other people in your class</u>. You'll need to <u>process</u> and <u>analyse</u> all the data you have. This might involve a few different things:

1) <u>Displaying</u> and <u>organising</u> the data using <u>tables</u>.
2) Carrying out mathematical <u>calculations</u> to <u>process</u> the data.
3) Drawing <u>graphs</u> or <u>diagrams</u> to <u>display</u> the data.
4) Looking for <u>patterns</u> in the now beautifully presented data.

Data **Needs to be** Organised

1) Data that's been collected needs to be <u>organised</u> so it can be processed — <u>tables</u> are dead useful for this.
2) Tables are also good for spotting any <u>outliers</u> (see page 3) — you'll need to have spotted these so you can account for them when you're <u>concluding</u> and <u>evaluating</u> later.
3) When drawing tables, make sure that <u>each column</u> has a <u>heading</u> and that you've included the <u>units</u>.

Data **Can be** Processed **Using a Bit of** Maths

1) <u>Raw data</u> generally just ain't that useful. You usually have to <u>process</u> it in some way.
2) A couple of the most simple calculations you can perform are the <u>mean</u> (average) and the <u>range</u> (how spread out the data is):

- To calculate the <u>mean</u> <u>ADD TOGETHER</u> all the data values and <u>DIVIDE</u> by the total number of values. You usually do this to get a single value from several <u>repeats</u> of your experiment.

- To calculate the <u>range</u> find the <u>LARGEST</u> number and <u>SUBTRACT</u> the <u>SMALLEST</u> number. You usually do this to <u>check</u> how precise your results are when you've taken repeated readings. Precise results are ones where the data is <u>all really close</u> to the <u>mean</u> (i.e. not spread out). The <u>greater</u> the <u>spread</u> of the data, the <u>lower</u> the reliability of the results.

Different Types **of** Data **Should be** Presented **in** Different Ways

1) You'll need to <u>present</u> your data so that it's easier to see <u>patterns</u> and <u>relationships</u> in the data.
2) Different types of investigations give you <u>different types</u> of data, so you'll always have to <u>choose</u> what the best way to present your data is.

Bar Charts

If the independent variable is <u>categoric</u> (comes in distinct categories, e.g. blood types, metals) you should use a <u>bar chart</u> to display the data. You also use them if the independent variable is <u>discrete</u> (the data can be counted in chunks, where there's no in-between value, e.g. number of people is discrete because you can't have half a person).

There are some <u>golden rules</u> you need to follow for <u>drawing</u> bar charts:

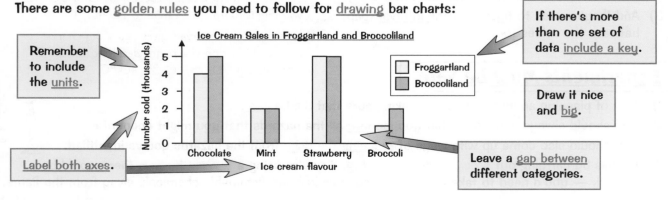

Remember to include the <u>units</u>.

Label both axes.

If there's more than one set of data <u>include a key</u>.

Draw it nice and <u>big</u>.

Leave a <u>gap between</u> different categories.

Processing the Data

Hold up, you haven't finished with <u>data processing</u> yet, and there's still the <u>analysis</u> to think about. Sheesh.

Line Graphs

If the independent variable is <u>continuous</u> (numerical data that can have any value within a range, e.g. length, volume, temperature) you should use a <u>line graph</u> to display the data.

Use the biggest data values you've got to draw a <u>sensible scale</u> on your axes. For example, the highest rate of reaction is <u>22 cm³/s</u>, so it makes sense to label the y-axis up to <u>25 cm³/s</u>.

The <u>dependent</u> variable goes on the <u>y-axis</u> (the <u>vertical</u> one).

The <u>independent</u> variable goes on the <u>x-axis</u> (the <u>horizontal</u> one).

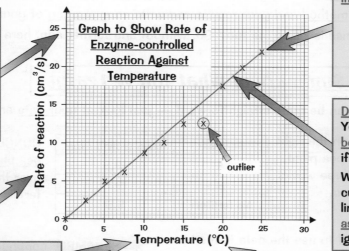

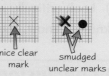

When plotting points, use a <u>sharp pencil</u> and make a <u>neat little cross</u> (don't do blobs).

nice clear mark

smudged unclear marks

<u>Don't join the dots up</u>. You should draw a <u>line of best fit</u> (or a <u>curve of best fit</u> if your points make a curve).

When drawing a line (or curve), try to draw the line <u>through</u> or as <u>near</u> to <u>as many points as possible</u>, ignoring any outliers.

Remember to include the <u>units</u>.

Graphs <u>Can Give You a Lot of Information About Your Data</u>

If you've presented your data in a graph, you can use it to show a <u>bit more</u> about the data or even do some <u>calculations</u>.
For example, if 'time' is on the x-axis, you can calculate the <u>gradient</u> (<u>slope</u>) of the line to find the <u>rate of reaction</u>:

1) Gradient = y ÷ x

2) You can calculate the gradient of the <u>whole line</u> or a <u>section</u> of it.

3) The rate would be in <u>cm³/s</u>.

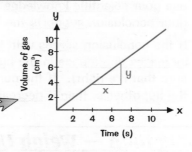

Line Graphs <u>Can Show Relationships in Data</u>

Before you can make any conclusions, you need to look for <u>patterns</u> or <u>relationships</u> between variables.

1) <u>Line graphs</u> are great for showing relationships between two variables.

2) Here are the <u>three</u> different types of <u>correlation</u> (relationship) shown on line graphs:

There's more on correlation on page 4.

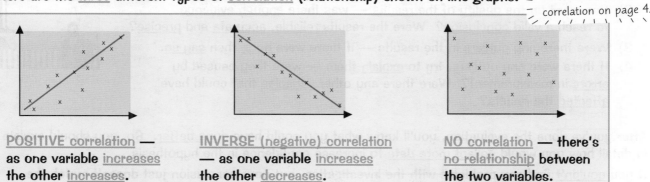

<u>POSITIVE correlation</u> — as one variable <u>increases</u> the other <u>increases</u>.

<u>INVERSE (negative) correlation</u> — as one variable <u>increases</u> the other <u>decreases</u>.

<u>NO correlation</u> — there's <u>no relationship</u> between the two variables.

3) Remember, don't <u>confuse correlation</u> with <u>cause</u> — there might be <u>other factors</u> involved (see page 4).

Controlled Assessment

Conclusion and Evaluation

At the end of your practical investigation, the <u>conclusion</u> and <u>evaluation</u> will be waiting.
Don't worry, they won't bite. Here's what you'll need to do:

1) Draw a <u>conclusion</u> from your primary data.

2) <u>Compare</u> the secondary data with the primary data. Say whether the secondary data <u>agrees</u> or <u>disagrees</u> with your conclusion from the primary data.

3) Look back at the <u>hypothesis</u> and say how well it's <u>supported</u> by your conclusion and secondary data.

4) Look critically at your <u>method</u> and your <u>results</u> and write an <u>evaluation</u> of your investigation.

I know, I know, the suspense is killing me too. So, without any further ado, here are the finer details...

A Conclusion is a Summary of What You've Learnt

1) Drawing a conclusion can be quite straightforward — just <u>look at your data</u> and <u>say what pattern you see</u>.

EXAMPLE: The table on the right shows the heights of pea plant seedlings grown for three weeks with different fertilisers.

Fertiliser	Mean growth / mm
A	13.5
B	19.5
No fertiliser	5.5

<u>CONCLUSION</u>: Fertiliser <u>B</u> makes <u>pea plant</u> seedlings grow taller over the first <u>three weeks</u> than fertiliser A.

2) However, you also need to use the data that's been <u>collected</u> to <u>justify</u> the conclusion (back it up).

EXAMPLE continued... Over the three weeks, fertiliser B made the pea plants grow 6 mm more on average than fertiliser A.

3) There are some things to watch out for too — it's important that the conclusion <u>matches the data</u> it's based on and <u>doesn't go any further</u>.

EXAMPLE continued... You can't conclude that fertiliser B makes <u>any other type of plant</u> grow taller than fertiliser A — the results could be totally different. Also, you can't make any conclusions <u>beyond</u> the three weeks — the plants could <u>drop dead</u>.

4) You then need to look back at the <u>hypothesis</u> and use your <u>scientific knowledge</u> to explain how well your conclusion <u>supports</u> the hypothesis.

5) If the conclusion <u>agrees</u> with the hypothesis, then it <u>increases confidence</u> in the hypothesis (makes us more sure that it's right). If the conclusion <u>doesn't agree</u> with the hypothesis, then it <u>decreases confidence</u> in the hypothesis (makes us less sure that it's right).

Evaluation — Weigh Up How Well Things Went

An evaluation is a <u>critical analysis</u> — be honest and point out the <u>problems</u> with your investigation.

1) Comment on the <u>method</u> — you should say if there were any <u>problems</u> with the method (e.g. with the techniques or apparatus you used), then you should say how it could be <u>improved</u>.

2) Comment on the <u>quality</u> of the <u>results</u> — was there <u>enough evidence</u> to reach a valid <u>conclusion</u>? Were the results <u>reliable</u>, <u>accurate</u> and <u>precise</u>?

3) Were there any <u>outliers</u> in the results — if there were <u>none</u> then <u>say so</u>.

4) If there were any outliers, try to <u>explain</u> them — were they caused by <u>errors</u> in measurement? Were there any other <u>variables</u> that could have <u>affected</u> the results?

After you've done the evaluation, you'll know what you could have <u>done better</u>. So, you should explain in detail how you would <u>collect more data</u> to increase confidence in the hypothesis.

If you <u>couldn't</u> find any problems with the investigation, but your conclusion just doesn't match the hypothesis, then you should suggest <u>alterations</u> you could make to the hypothesis so that it <u>matches</u> your conclusion. You could then suggest ways to test the new hypothesis with <u>further experiments</u>.

Index

A

accuracy (of data) 77

active transport 42, 47

adaptations (of organisms) 29

ADH (anti-diuretic hormone) 27

adult stem cells 15, 52

aerobic respiration 42

alleles 8-10

amino acids 49

  synthesis of 42, 44

ammonia 36

anaerobic respiration 43

animal cells 40

animal development 52

antagonistic muscles 65

antibiotics 20, 70

  resistance to 20

antibodies 18

antigens 18

antimicrobials 20

  resistance to 20

aorta 22

arteries 22

asexual reproduction 14

auxins 54

average (mean) 3, 77, 78

axons 57

B

bacterial cells 40

bar charts 78

bases (DNA) 49

behaviour 60, 61

bioaccumulation 74

biodiversity 32

biofuels 70

biogas 43

biomedical engineering 72

blind trials 21

blood 64

  cells 64

  pressure 23, 66

  sugar level (control of) 69

  vessels 22

BMI (body mass index) 66

body temperature (control of) 68

brain 56

  development 60, 61

  study of the 62

bulbs (plants) 14

C

capillaries 22, 65

carbon cycle 35

cartilage 65

cause (of relationships between variables) 4, 79

cell

  division 50, 51

  membranes 40

  specialisation 52

  structures 40

  walls 40

central nervous system (CNS) 56, 58

cerebral cortex 61

chlorophyll 40, 44

chloroplasts 40

chromosomes 8, 50, 51

circulatory system 22, 64

classification (of organisms) 32

clinical trials 21

clones 14

cloning 52

closed loop systems 74

competition 33

conclusions 80

conditioned reflexes 59

controlled assessment 77-80

core body temperature 68

coronary arteries 22

correlations 4, 79

cuttings (plant) 53

cystic fibrosis 12

cytoplasm 40

D

Darwin, Charles 31

data 3, 78, 79

decomposers 34-36

denitrifying bacteria 36

detritivores 34

diabetes 69

diffusion 47

dislocations 67

DNA 8, 49-51

dominant alleles 10, 12

double-blind trials 21

drugs

  affecting synapses 57

  side effects of 19, 21

  trials of 21

E

ecosystems 73-75

  conservation of 75

  stability of 73, 74

ecstasy (MDMA) 57

effectors 25, 56, 58

electrical impulses 57

embryonic stem cells 15, 52

energy transfer (in ecosystems) 34

environmental changes 37

environmental damage 6

enzymes 41

  industrial production of 70

epidemics 19

epidemiological studies 24

equipment (for experiments) 77

ethics 7

eutrophication 74

evaluations 80

evidence (from experiments) 1

Index

Index

Index and Answers

Answers

Revision Summary for Module B1 (page 16)

11)

| parents' phenotypes: | Loves Aston Villa | Loves Aston Villa |

parents' genotypes: **AA**   **Aa**

sex cells' genotypes: **A** **A**   **A** **a**

possible genotypes of offspring: **AA** **AA** **Aa** **Aa**

All the offspring love Aston Villa, but half of them carry the allele for being normal.

12)

Parent who loves Aston Villa

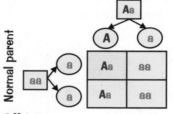

Offspring:
Two **Aa** genotypes so half the offspring will love Aston Villa. Two **aa** genotypes, so the other half of the offspring will be normal.

Revision Summary for Module B2 (page 28)

3)   6 hours = 360 mins
360 ÷ 40 = 9 reproduction periods:
1) 1 x 2 = 2
2) 2 x 2 = 4
3) 4 x 2 = 8
4) 8 x 2 = 16
5) 16 x 2 = 32
6) 32 x 2 = 64
7) 64 x 2 = 128
8) 128 x 2 = 256
9) 256 x 2 = 512 bacteria.
or 2^9 = 512 bacteria.

26) a) Dave because he has a more stressful job than Tricia / he smokes / he does less exercise than Tricia / he has a diet higher in saturated fats and salt than Tricia.

b) Improve your diet, e.g. eat less fatty foods and salt / be less stressed / stop smoking / don't use drugs like ecstasy and cannabis / reduce the amount of alcohol you consume / do regular moderate exercise.

Revision Summary for Module B5 (page 55)

10)

	Mitosis	Meiosis
Its purpose is to provide new cells for growth and repair.	✓	✗
Its purpose is to create gametes (sex cells).	✗	✓
The cells produced are genetically identical.	✓	✗
The cells produced contain half the number of chromosomes that were in the parent cell.	✗	✓